Star's Miracles and More

Rosemary Gustafson

Star's Miracles and More
by Rosemary Gustafson

Printed in the United States of America

ISBN 9781619044944

Unless otherwise indicated, Bible quotations are taken from The New King James Version.

Photography by: Ragnar Gustafson

Cover design: Ragnar and Rosemary Gustafson, Janie McQueen, and Xulon Press

www.xulonpress.com

Table of Contents

O MIGHTY HORSE

O MIGHTY HORSE,
  created of God,
  by man and beast you are held in awe.
Your feet are held in the Master's hand,
  enabled to run on sod or sand.
Your awesome beauty— your head held high,
  with nostrils flaring—charging!
   to the battles' cry.
Many are the wars that are won from your back:
  truth and courage you do not lack.
We are blessed of God— by having such as you
  may God find us all so faithful and true.

O MIGHTY HORSE! created of God
  you— yes— you are the vehicle of our Lord.
O mighty horse— what honor bestows you:
  to be ridden by One called Faithful and True.
The King of Kings and LORD of LORDS:
  O mighty horse— he'll be mounted on you.
Swiftly you will come in the clouds on that day
  in this one last battle— you've a big part to play.
Once again there will be peace in the land
  O MIGHTY HORSE— you're a part of God's plan.

D.J. JONES

Used by permission of the author, Diane Jones

Foreword

I remember back to the day when I was laying prostrate on the floor in the family room, with my nose in the rug, bawling, crying and praying for my Dalmatian dog, Amie. She was in Whatcom Veterinary Hospital with a poisoned pancreas and very critically ill. Tubes were running into her to keep her alive. I was a basket case!

With tears steaming down my face, I all of a sudden stopped sobbing and began to think. What am I doing? I have a friend whose child is battling cancer and people all over the world are suffering. Japan had a terrible earthquake and people were killed and missing. Their homes were destroyed in the earthquake. What am I doing praying for a dog? Then that still small voice inside said, "Do not compare yourself to anyone else. I love you as though you are my only child." I sat up and just marveled in awe. God loves me as though I were His only child! He does not compare me to anyone else or other situations. Then I realized that whatever is important to me He cares about. The God of Abraham, Isaac, and Jacob is a God of love and He cares about everyone individually – right where you are! He cares about His creation. Three days later my dog recovered and all of the tubes were removed. I brought her home, thanking God for hearing my prayers.

I learned a very powerful lesson about God's love that day on the rug. Do I understand all of it? No, but I believe it by **faith** because the Bible says that He is a God of love. Does that mean that we can just go out and do anything because of that love? There are always consequences when you disobey God and make bad choices. The good news is that He is also a God of mercy, grace and forgiveness when anyone comes to Him with a heart of repentance! What does all this have to do with a story about a horse? It tells my story of a God Who cares about my horses, dogs and life situations. He wants to be involved with everything in my life. God wants to be involved in all of **your** lives. His desire is to fellowship with you not just on Sunday morning from the church pew or at meals times, but, all the time. He wants a **relationship**.

Hebrews 13:5 says "He will never leave you or forsake you." So He is always there - just talk to Him. You have a direct line and God is never too busy!

Psalm 139:3 "You (God) comprehend my path and my lying down and are INTIMATELY acquainted with ALL my ways"

Endorsements

Rosemary Gustafson lives what she writes. Her prophetic gifting breaks through the walls of religion into the horse lover's world. Her insight into God's kingdom reveals power and love, integrity and victory. Her book illustrates God working through our horses to expand His kingdom. The relationship of horse and rider is a living picture of the believer's relationship with the Lord Jesus Christ. In the read, I had amazing encounters with the Spirit of the Lord! This real story helps young and old become as God's mighty horse in battle. Mount up and ride triumphantly in His Majesty in Rosemary's book!

Coy Huffman
Pro Rodeo Ministers
Cowboy Church International, Inc.

Rosemary's stories of tenacious courage will warm your heart. I cried, laughed and rose up in indignation as she led me through Star's journey. This book will encourage and inspire you to reach out to the Lord even in the little things in life.

Rosemary truly is an amazing woman full of faith and hope. I know you, too, will be filled with the same faith and hope when reading this remarkable book.

Pastor Carolyn Steidley

The Glory Riders of California.

Acknowledgments

T hanks to my editor, Janie McQueen, who has always been there encouraging me and spurring me on when it all seemed too overwhelming to me. She spent the extra hours beyond what an editor is asked to do.

Thanks to my husband, Ragnar, who has always walked beside me in the good times of joy and laughter, and was also there in times of tears and sadness.

Thanks to our children Heidi, Leif, Erik, Tiffany, Shay and Ryan, who lived much of the story and all have their own memories of Star and her battle for life.

Thanks to Carol Dawson our dear freind who never stopped praying for me and the book. She caught the vision of my heart to share with others the love of the Lord in an intimate relationship. To encourage other people that God loves them and wants to be involved with their daily lives.

Thanks to all my other friends who prayed and all the gals I ride with, Lori Hunt, Sue Stacy and especially Merilee Erchinger who, at a time when I was questioning what I was even doing writing a book, took the rough draft of the book and read it while we were camping. She came to me at the end of camp week crying and thanking me for writing the book. I was astonished and once again was spurred on that this really was God.

Thanks to all the veterinarians, Dr. Kent Freer of Whidbey Island, Wa. and all the veterinarians at Kulshan Hospital in Lynden and my wonderful son-in-law Dr. Terry Beatty who all had a part in either Star or Amies life.

Also, thanks to Dr. Sharon Hoofnagle who has recently been involved with some health issues that Star is going through at 30 years old. Her care and input for Star has been very much appreciated.

Above all thanks be to God because with out Him there would be no story or miracle of hope, joy and His love. It is really God who inspired me to write this book about Star and the other stories. I am not a natural writer. I am a cowgirl at heart and love the outdoors, horses, dogs and Gods creation - so it had to come from Him!

CHAPTER 1

"A Star is born"

Philippians 4:19 "And my God shall supply all your need according to His riches in glory by Christ Jesus."

S o much was going on in my life when this beautiful filly was born, that I don't remember much about her birth. But, it was a small beginning that made a huge impact on my life, our entire family's life and others, too. She is living proof that God cares about all of His creation because she has had so many wonderful miracles in her life!

My head was in the clouds because I was getting married for the second time and together we had six kids – four boys and two girls - ages six to thirteen. I do remember some of the kids wanting to sleep in the barn so they could see the foal's birth. But, as I recall, we all missed most of it. There is something very special about a new life, but for me it's the birth of a horse. For one thing, I think God likes barns because His Son was born in one. I also like the smell of new straw, the miracle of those long legs all getting out, and the struggle to get them working so the foal can stand. I can sense the presence of the Lord in the barn when a baby horse is born. It's an awesome and wonderful feeling!

I don't remember anything very unusual about this little bay filly with the star on her forehead and four white socks, but she has become a very unique and special horse. Now, we call her the miracle horse, because of all she has been through and the prayers to God for her.

CHAPTER 2

"Homeless"

Matthew 6:31 "Therefore do not worry, saying, what shall we eat or what shall we drink or wear? .... for your heavenly Father knows that you need all of these things."

Do you remember the TV show "The Brady Bunch"? That's pretty much what our family was like, except that I didn't get the maid, Alice. However, unlike the TV show, we had some ups and a lot of tragic downs, so we ended up a homeless family of eight!

After a few months into our new marriage, we had moved to an island with the idea of becoming a unified, blended family. The island was beautiful and the kids all loved it and grew close, because it was a very small community. Don't be mistaken, because becoming a blended family is NOT easy. Only with the help of God, His love and His wisdom were we able to survive. But, that's another story! During this time on the island, my husband's company on the mainland was having financial problems, as were most businesses in the early 80's, and we ended up losing everything. First, the vehicles were taken and then his business property. We had a twin-engine airplane that the bank simply moved without any notification or telling us! They also confiscated a beautiful lodge we had in Canada that we fought to keep, but lost. We, who had nothing, were trying to fight a very big bank which had a lot of money and we had none. I had six horses, very little income and needed to feed six kids - let alone the horses!

But, we had many miracles during this time. Bags of food would miraculously appear on our doorstep and a check would arrive just in time to stop the electricity from being turned off. This was a time in our lives when all of us knew that God was taking care of us in many ways, and with the love of so many people. Some people knew us and some didn't even know who we were! One time, a man on the island who I did not know, called and asked if my kids were in 4-H. Yes, they were, so he gave us a barn full of hay for our horses. That hay lasted all winter and then I was able to sell two horses.

I learned many things during the hard times of losing everything, but one thing for sure is that there is a God who cares and uses people to show His love for us. I also learned that things can be replaced, but family and friends are forever. They are the true treasures of life.

Then, we were given notice that we had to vacate our home. A month before we were to move someone called and asked if I would like to put my horses on their 20 acres (pasture) for the summer. The people needed it eaten down. I had no idea what I would have done with the horses if this pasture had not come up. I was not sure how a family of eight was going to survive or the four horses! It was not too far from a friend who said she'd make sure the horses had water and she'd be able to watch out for them.

So we left the island, homeless, and moved in with my husband's brother who was a bachelor living in a cabin on a small lake. We had to farm some of the kids out to friends because his home was very small.

I thought I was in a bad dream. This only happened to other people. How could this have happened to us? We were hard working people. We had just lost everything, and life looked dim. Except for the hope we had in Jesus. And the hope we had in the goodness of God's people, and the hope I had in a very hard working husband who is always so positive about everything.

It was my husband who found a home to rent on an ocean beach front. Most people did not want to rent to a family with six kids, but this man was desperate – so he let us rent it with an option to buy, and then he was gone. The miracle of this part of the story is that we were just a homeless family with nothing and within 10 years we had purchased this beautiful beach home and paid it off in full. Believe me, that was God! We also were able to fence in 15 acres to use for pasture (this was for free) just behind us for my horses. And, there was a two stall barn, two paddocks and a small fenced ring to ride in on our beach property. Coupled with all that - the pasture was perfect!

CHAPTER 3

"The Storm"

Ecclesiastes 3:1-4 "To everything there is a season, a time for every purpose under heaven. A time to be born, and a time to die…a time to kill, and a time to heal…time to laugh: a time to mourn, and a time to dance."

The night of the storm seemed like any other night. We were eating in the formal dining room because it overlooked the ocean. All of us were there and I am sure we were laughing and talking. All of a sudden there was a terrible crash like a bomb! The pictures moved on the walls and the dishes clattered in the cupboards. We really didn't see the lightning strike. At that point, we weren't sure what had happened until I got a phone call that one of my horses was walking down the road with blood all over her. My heart skipped a beat, and I yelled to my family that something had happened to the horses!

We raced for our car and as many could fit jumped in and we drove to the pasture behind our place. My beautiful filly, Star, was staggering around dazed. I got a halter and caught her. Then I saw that most of her chest and front legs looked like hamburger!

Frantically, we called the veterinarian, Dr. Freer. He was a solid old vet who took care of everything on four legs in that area and had 'been there and done that' when it came to treating animals. He also volunteered as a missionary veterinarian and would go overseas to help third world countries with their livestock. I am sure he had seen nearly everything when caring for animals.

By this time we had found two of our other horses and they seemed fine. But, a full sister to Star, who was a gorgeous dark bay filly turning grey, we could not find.

The fire department was called because of the huge explosion that we soon discovered was a tree that the lightning had hit. It literally exploded and split in two! Lights were flashing and people coming, but we still had not found the filly.

Dr. Freer looked at Star's injuries and his face told the story - it was very serious. My head was spinning and we had not even found the filly yet. Dr. Freer said Star would probably not be able to use the very badly damaged front leg, even after sewing it all back together. The Doc knew she was a very well bred Arab. So, he said she would probably drag that leg and not be able to use it, but she could be a broodmare and have great babies. I was trying to process this and all I could think of was to just save her life.

Yes, Dr. Freer was very right, because Star is a triple Witez II great granddaughter. In case you don't know who Witez II is, he was the foundation stallion for most of the Polish Arabian horse bred in America. Today, there are few descendants of Witez II and Star is one of them!

A little history of Witez II and how General Patten got involved with him began in 1938 when a small band of yearling horses was taken from the rest of their herd so that they would be easier to handle. This was done because Adolph Hitler's Nazi troops had invaded Poland and absolutely no horse was exempt from becoming a 'spoil of war'. It was greatly hoped that they would be safe somewhere to the east so, as a group, the yearlings began their pilgrimage to the only escape from the German army. It was then that this frightening journey began.

A dark bay Arab colt named Witez II (meaning "The Prince") was among the band as it moved on foot across the land. German bombers appeared above the horses and the planes commenced dropping bombs into the field where the horses were crossing! You can imagine the panic of the horses, and though Witez II's handler was able to regain control over the animal, they were separated from the others and forced to continue alone.

Being by yourself was very frightening, because travel alone during those times was scary and difficult. Eventually, the horse's handler found safety with a local woodcutter who used the horse to help him haul lumber. After it became too dangerous to remain with the woodcutter, they bravely departed. Witez II was developing into quite a quality horse, so the handler smeared the animal's hair with mud to disguise him.

It was then that the pair went to Janow, hoping to have access to some of the precious feed in the stables. Janow, being occupied by the Germans, had feed only at the stables where the studs were kept. Witez's handler crept into the stables each night and stole food for his horse, but the amount he was able to get wasn't enough. Because the handler feared for Witez's life, he reluctantly gave the horse to the Germans, asking them to restore his health.

Not common knowledge at that time, Nazi Germany had a secret program to breed a "super horse" to carry the Nazi army of "super men" into battle. And an evaluation of Witez II convinced the Germans that the animal was indeed of high quality and should join 1500 horses of different breeds in Hostau, Czechoslovakia, where the breeding program was initiated.

Shortly after Witez II was moved to Czechoslovakia, the Americans and Russians began advancing dangerously close to the Hostau stud ranch. Concerned for the safety of their special

horses, Dr. R Lessing, DVM (veterinarian) in charge of the program, was fearful that the Russians might capture their horses and butcher them for food. So, he and an associate traveled through enemy lines with a white flag of surrender, speaking English words learned from a German-English dictionary *and asked the Americans for help. "Wonder-horses," he told the Americans, "all good horses...super-horses." General George Patton Jr. then gave permission to negotiate for the animals to be surrendered.*

The German army didn't want to give up their "super-horses" peacefully and General Patton had to "liberate" the animals as "prisoners of war" before the Russians arrived. Despite the ease of the capture of Hostau, two American platoons with the horses were cut off from the Americans and were forced to wait for reinforcements.

It was on April 28, 1945 that the "super-horses" were ridden out of Hostau by the Americans. It was two hundred miles farther and they were under fire while riding to Bavaria. Though many of the horses were lame, not one had been lost. The horses were then taken to Monsback Stud to be cared for by General Patton's best horseman. After checking each horse's lineage, the General made arrangements for them to go to the United States on a freighter to the U.S. Army Remount Station at Front Royal, Virginia.

Heavy seas in the middle of winter caused the journey to be longer than originally planned and the constant moisture of being at sea turned the horse's hay in storage moldy. Many horses colicked, yet Witez II completed the journey in fairly good condition. He even bred the mare Iwonka III, who gave birth to Wontez.

When the ship reached Virginia, Witez II was sent to the Army Remount Service, where he was a stud until the US government determined in 1949 that "a horse was no longer a necessary vehicle of war". Witez II was then sold at auction and joined many horses at Hurlbutt Calarabia Ranch in California. It was there that he lived the rest of his years and enjoyed life as a stud horse. Witez II sired hundreds of foals and some of them went on to be champions. He died quietly in his pasture in 1965.

Though horse shows were relatively new in America, Witez II was the 1951 Grand Champion at the Southern California All Arabian Show (one of the largest) in Pomona and at the age of 15, he was the Pacific Coast Champion Stallion and Overall Grand Champion in 1953. These championships were great awards for Arabian horses.

Witez II earned the respect of Arabian breeders because of his incredible story and he owes his great success as a stud horse to a "look of eagles" that he maintained throughout all the hardships he endured. His story has been written in two books and Witez II also had his image recreated on a Polish postage stamp.

It is said that Witez II is responsible for the Polish Arabian's legacy in America and that's quite a princely accomplishment!" Though Star was a decendant of Witez II, her sire (father) was also a spectacular stallion whose name was Shabaoud. He was a beautiful, brilliant, red, chestnut Arabian horse who carried himself like a king. He won in the Arabian horse shows at the halter class and also under saddle. He was never beaten in the 'Most Classic Class'. He was so loved by his owners, Paul and Joy Manning and

Wayne and Karen Storkel that the night Shabaoud passed away, Karen spent the night in his stall and he died with his head in Karen's arms. He was a ripe old age, too!

Meanwhile, they found the filly. She was lying down and not getting up, which meant she was very seriously injured. Another veterinarian was also on the scene. He found her and was not sure if she was just stunned and in shock or if her back or neck was broken. The veterinarian with the filly said we would just have to watch her to see if she attempted to get up. He also instructed us that she must be turned over every hour or so because a horse cannot lie down flat for an extended period of time. So that meant someone would have to take turns turning her over from side to side. That isn't an easy thing to do with a horse because you must get hold of the legs and pull the horse over - hoping they don't kick you! Word travels fast in a small community and friends appeared at our disaster scene, volunteering to help. We took them up on their offer and they ended up staying all night, helping to turn the filly over and over.

By 9:00 p.m., the fire department had set up special lights for Dr. Freer so he could clean the wounds on Star. After he cleaned the wounds, he began to suture her. I don't remember exactly how many stitches the doctor needed to do internally just trying to bring the hamburger mess together - but it was in the hundreds. Then after what felt like hours and hours he began stitching the ghastly looking injury on the outside of poor Star. My husband and our six children watched (it was like a horror movie) as firemen, veterinarians and friends all worked together to help these animals survive. When Doctor Freer was finished stitching Star, he took me aside and said again that he doubted if she would have any use in that front leg because the tendons and ligaments were damaged so badly. He also added that it would be a very long recuperation time and require much doctoring to keep any *proud flesh* from growing.

Proud flesh is the result of granulated tissue which normally fills in a deeply lacerated or punctured injury and when too much of it is produced, it causes the tissue to bulge out around the area of the wound. This keeps the skin edges from healing together. If the *proud flesh* cannot be controlled by either pressure wraps or rubbing with antibiotic ointment, it must be surgically removed. *Proud flesh* usually occurs only on the legs and Star's front leg was a mess from the knee up and all over her chest. She would have to be confined to a stall for many months and doctored twice a day by cleaning and rubbing the wound to stop any *proud flesh* from taking over.

My mouth was saying yes, but my mind was asking "How are you going to do this?" I am *not* a vet and those wounds looked really scary!

Dr. Freer continued to come and check on her and showed me how to scrub the wounds. He convinced me that it was not hurting Star to rub the wounds by telling me that horses skin is not as sensitive as ours. That's not true, but it worked, because I believed him and scrubbed those wounds like a woman washing clothes on a washboard! Each time I scrubbed and doctored her I also prayed and asked God to mend all the tendons and ligaments. She was confined to a stall for several months and God was so faithful because Star regained full use of the leg that she was suppose to only be able to drag!

That began the first of many miracles that followed this beautiful and sensitive bay mare with the star on her forehead and four white socks.

Her full sister, the other filly, did not fare so well. My family and friends took turns turning her over all night, but she was no better the following morning. The vet came out that same morning to examine her and felt, at this point, that she must have broken her back. So, with a heavy heart and eyes full of tears, I gave the vet permission to put her to sleep.

My whole night had been such a state of shock and trauma. The cause of all this was a lightning bolt that hit a tree where Star and her sister were standing. As I said before, the tree literally exploded and split into two pieces. Someone took a picture and it was in the newspaper that week. Even to think of the photograph brings back horrifying memories.

CHAPTER 4

"Stolen"

Psalm 37:23 "The steps of a righteous man are guided by the Lord"

The next year when Star turned three, she was completely healed and had no lameness at all. In fact, she moved like a deer - graceful and fluid. But, she did have a horrible scar down her chest and front leg that told the story of a horrible injury. I decided to begin training her for riding. She was so smart and seemed to always be one step ahead of me. She was always kind, but very quick. I actually put my daughter Tiffany on her as the first rider. Star was very good, but a lot of horse for a young rider. My farrier (horseshoer) told me about a lady who lived 50 miles away and loved Arabs, who might be interested in training Star. I got a hold of this lady and spent quite a bit of time questioning her and getting to know her on the phone. She actually wanted to lease Star and that worked well for both of us – or so I thought at the time! The lady leased Star for two years and I called her many, many times just to check on how she and the horse were doing. She was really enjoying Star as her own riding horse. Things seemed to be going very well. She wanted to extend the free lease and I had no problem with extending the lease because I didn't have much time for another horse right now because my family took all my time and energy.

I was busy being a 'horse show mom' - brush and cleaning cloth in hand to wipe the dust and any spots of dirt off the horse before my daughter went into the show ring. We went from show to show and we had a blast! My daughter, Tiffany, was winning and I was so proud of her. Those years were full of horse shows, basketball, soccer and football games for six kids. Trying to keep up with all their activities was a full plate and I seemed to be stretched in all directions. There were also many emotional needs created by an earlier divorce that only God can heal. To renew the lease of one horse seemed like a small and necessary task and nothing to be greatly concerned with.

I spent hours sitting in the bleachers or on the side lines yelling and screaming for our kids and their teams. I quickly learned to bring a pillow for the hard wooden benches on which I spent most of my time! *But, I did not have time to think about my beautiful bay mare with a star on her forehead.* My life was full of kids.

It was at this time that we had a friend over and she was looking at our pictures around the house. Noticing a picture of Star, she said that the horse looked just like "so and so's" horse and I told her that the same lady had leased my horse. My friends face took on a shocked look and she said, "That lady has left the county with that horse and one other horse that she stole!" The word 'stole' went bouncing around in my mind. Horse thief - no - that only happened in the old cowboy days, not today. I inquired, "Are you sure?" She quickly answered, "Yes, the other people were trying to get their stolen horse back and it was quite a mess. At this time, no one knows where she has gone."

I felt sick. My beautiful mare, Star, was stolen. How could that have happened? I didn't need that! My head was floundering - what on earth do you do to catch a horse thief?

My friend, who lived in the same area where my horse was stolen, said she would find out every thing she could and we kept in touch by phone constantly. Finally, my friend had a lead on Star. Someone said they recognized the horse because that was the horse the thief had listed for sale - on the other side of the state!

I called about the horse and, sure enough, she was at a place in Omak, Washington. I got the address and my husband and I were on our way with our horse trailer in tow.

And, I don't mind saying that it was with the 'spirit of Roy Rogers to the rescue' that we left. If you don't know who Roy Rogers was, he was my childhood cowboy hero, with his beautiful palamino horse, Trigger. He always got the bad guy and taught children to obey their parents, love their country, and to love God.

So, we crossed the Cascade Mountains very early and arrived at the farm that morning. Then, we were greeted by the most colorful cowboy character I have ever seen! He looked just like one of those cowboys on a greeting card with a prickly face and funny old cowboy hat and shirt. He was so bow-legged that I wondered how he could even walk! His voice was as gruff as he looked. I told him who I was looking for and he growled back at me that she had taken her horses and moved out. My heart sank to by boots. I turned and walked away.

Before I got to the truck I felt the Lord saying to me, "You go back there and tell that cowboy the truth about Star." So I turned around and started back to face the old cowboy. As I did the tears began to flow from my eyes and in a very broken voice between sobs, I said to the old cowboy, "That lady has stolen my horse and I was hoping to find her here." Just then something magical happened to that ruff-tuff old cowboy, because he turned into my knight in shining armor! Putting his arm around me, he spoke very tenderly, "Don't you worry, little lady, I'll help you get that horse back." And he did! The old cowboy continued, "Let me give you the phone number of my lawyer". At the word 'lawyer' my mind began to see dollar signs and money spent that I didn't have. But, I was hopeless and ready to try anything to get Star back.

So, with the lawyer's business card in hand, we headed across the state to Davenport, WA. where he thought she had moved. My instructions were to call the lawyer when we got to Davenport. So, now we were heading even farther across the state to find my little mare, Star.

Arriving in Davenport in the late afternoon, I called the lawyer. To my surprise he was very nice. And, the old cowboy had already called him about our mission to find my stolen horse. The lawyer had contacted the police department and they had done a search for the horse thief because she already had moved from Davenport. The police found her farther up in the northeast corner of Washington in a very small town. The towns are all small in that part of the country.

They also put me in touch with a brand inspector, who happened to be the Sheriff and was familiar with the lady we were tracking. I had all of Stars papers and the lease agreement, to boot!

We arrived in this very remote part of the state around 8:00 p.m. that evening and met with the Sheriff. He was very nice and knew the lady we were trying to find. It also sounded like there were other "situations" with her. The sheriff explained to us that we could not go on her property to get the horse unless she granted us permission. Otherwise, we would be trespassing to get our own horse!

So, the sheriff went down to talk to the lady and said that if he flashed his light, we could come down. So, we waited on the road, looking at her place and praying, "God please let her be cooperative for us."

It seemed like forever and it was beginning to get dark. My mind was thinking of all the negative things that could happen. Finally, the patrol car's light began to flash! We hopped in the truck and drove down her driveway. She greeted us and my husband, Ragnar, began to talk to her. The sheriff grabbed my arm, pulled me aside and said, "The horse is in that pasture - go get her now and get the *#@* out of here before she changes her mind!" So, with halter in hand I walked out to the pasture, saw her standing there and I called her name. "Star, it's me. I have come to take you home." As I walked up to her she turned her backside to me. Now, any other horse person would have been very offended if a horse did that because it's very rude and can be dangerous if the horse decided to kick. But, for me, it brought tears to my eyes because it meant she remembered me! You see, for those six months that I doctored her I would always go to her backside and scratch, because doctoring the front end was very painful and I wanted to do something that would feel good to her. It was a ritual. First the behind-scratching and then I'd scrub the wound. Then we'd end with the behind-scratching. She remembered me and I was ecstatic! I put the halter on my horse and led her into the trailer. Now Star was in my possession!

Off we went, but by now it was 10:00 p.m. We were all exhausted and in the middle of nowhere, so we decided the best thing would be to drive to Spokane and find a place to stay. After arriving in Spokane about midnight, we thought it might not be too good to try and stay in town with a horse in the trailer. So we drove right on through Spokane and went west on a smaller highway. There we found a motel with a huge parking lot and not many cars. We woke the manager up and got a room. I had lots of hay and water for Star and she was in a stock trailer, so we turned her loose to walk around for the night. Big mistake! The horse trailer was just outside our room and she indeed walked around, making a good deal of noise in the trailer all night long. I don't think any one got any sleep at all - anywhere in the motel! I know we didn't get any sleep. I kept worrying if she was okay, or if she was going to get into trouble loose in the trailer. My mind had all kinds of visions of things that could go wrong with a horse loose in a trailer. But, thank God, she was just fine in the morning and off we went on the last leg of the journey to bring my stolen horse home. Actually, I didn't bring Star home because I was concerned that the horse thief might try to take her out of the pasture. So, I boarded Star with a friend for a couple weeks.

During that time I did get a letter from a lawyer of the horse thief with a bill for $8,000.00! The letter explained that his client was billing me for training my horse. I called that lawyer's office and gave them the phone number of the cowboy's lawyer in Spokane and I have never heard from either one of them since!

We now had miracle #2 for Star because God helped me bring my stolen horse back home and He led us from 'place to place' all over the state!

CHAPTER 5

"Missouri Fox Trotters"

Psalm 37:4 "Delight in the Lord and He will give you the desire of your heart."

By now, time has been flying by and we only had one boy home and a big 4000 sq. ft. home on the beach. I really did not want to go back to teaching (I did that many years ago) but, I felt like I should be doing something to bring in some cash. So, I researched 'Bed and Breakfasts' because of the beautiful low-bank and sandy beach where we lived. We did a little fixing up, added more deck and a huge, party hot tub overlooking the San Juan Islands and Olympic Mountains. It was time to put our sign out and we were in business.

What a blast! My husband and I both loved it and thoroughly enjoyed meeting people from all over who would come to stay at our beach home B&B. One couple, on their honeymoon, had ridden bikes from Long Island across the U.S. to the island where we lived. They rode their bikes from shore to shore and then they flew back to Long Island, taking over a month to ride their bikes across America.

One time we had some guests from Missouri and I had just heard about a horse breed from Missouri that I didn't know anything about. So, I thought I would ask my guests if they knew anything about this kind of horse. It was called a Missouri Fox Trotter. I imagined that because of their name they must pull carts on the race track or something. Wrong! My guests explained that the Fox Trotters were bred to move in a very special way that was extremely comfortable and that the Missouri Fox Trotters normally had quiet dispositions. Then, they told me that these horses were used by the old-time circuit preachers to carry the Gospel throughout the Ozark Mountains and from town to town. The country doctors who rode horses and used buggies liked to use them, too. They also said that the early cowboys and ranchers looked for horses with this special gait called the Fox Trot because they were especially comfortable and could cover long distances. The Fox Trotter's back feet do not pound or hit the ground like other horses feet do, they slide into the ground so there is no impact to your body. Wow! That sounded great to me, especially the 'no impact to your body' part.

Now, there was a bee in my bonnet and I would like to get a Fox Trotter. No sore muscles when you ride sounds very good to me. The biggest problem is that Missouri is a very long way from Washington State!

I asked the girl who first told me about these wonderful, comfortable horses and she told me about a breeder in a town called Monroe here in Washington. So, I called the breeder Joan Emerson and she was a wonderful gal. I loved her immediately. My daughter was off to college so I decided to breed her Appaloosa mare to a black and white Fox Trotter stallion. This turned out to be more difficult than I imagined! I would bring the mare home thinking she was settled (pregnant) and she would turn up not settled. Then, I would take her back and they would try again. Finally, the mare got a bad infection and I had to bring her home. I thought it would be best to wait until the following year's breeding season before trying again.

By the next year, the breeder had changed her mind about breeding horses and had sold all her stallions! She was just training and boarding horses now. She still owed me some money for the breeding fee, so we decided that I would take one of her fillies instead of the cash. I came with my horse trailer and she had picked out a filly that she was willing to trade for the breeding fee, if I was willing to give her a little extra money. The horse was a bay and white six month old filly with the biggest, brightest, blue eyes I have ever seen! But the filly also had a very big, long head to hold those big, blue eyes. You see, I was used to my Arab babies with their beautifully sculptured, dainty heads, tea cup muzzles, and big, brown eyes - horses that looked like STAR. This long head was new to me, but, she was going to be my answer to 'no more sore body' when I rode.

So we put our arms around her behind and literally pushed her into the horse trailer. No problems! This little filly became one of God's amazing miracles to me, in more ways then one, and one of the best horses I have ever owned. I named her Mayim because in Hebrew it means 'living water' - because of her beautiful, blue eyes. She grew into her head and became a stunningly gorgeous bay and white horse with a flowing, long, white mane and tail. Mayim was breathtaking! She was kind, gentle, and so willing to do anything I asked of her. I showed her in many Fox Trotter shows and she always placed first or second. And, though not happy when showing (she would sometimes grind her teeth), she always did what we asked. People just loved her and would always come up to ask about her because of those big, bright, blue eyes and flowing, long, mane that came down to her front leg. Mayim loved the attention and she loved the people.

I do not remember exactly what was behind the next thing I did with my horses, but I ended up buying two more horses from the same breeder!

One was a gorgeous solid black gelding (castrated stallion) named Black Beauty. I also bought a very cute, little yearling stallion named Cisco. Cisco ended up being the most incredible sire! He left his kind, sweet personality on all his babies and they were all naturally gaited.

CHAPTER 6

"Wolves and Wild Horses"

Psalm 24:1 "The earth is the Lords and all its fullness, the world and those who dwell in it."

Now I remember why we decided to get a stallion Fox Trotter! We were toying with the idea of moving way up north into Canada and bringing this wonderful breed up there. We began looking in an area of British Columbia, where my husband had very fond memories, because of a hunting and fishing lodge he used to own in B.C. We looked at some beautiful places, but the doors to them always seemed to close. Then we found one place in a spectacular valley looking at a huge lake and snow-capped mountain.

We had friends who lived in this remote valley. John and Tracy are their names, and they took us on a horse packing trip a few years ago. What an incredible memory! We rode over a mountain pass that was at the 7,000 ft. elevation (an old Indian trail) and eventually ends up at the coast. It was not used by anyone now. The ride started at their home and we wound up the mountain, riding through old-growth fir trees. We were in the middle of a huge forest when the horse I was riding began to eerily whinny and even scream!

I asked John what was going on and he said, "We are in the middle of his wild herd and your horse is calling to them." I said, "I don't see horses or hear anything." But, John said, "Your horse can smell them and knows they are in the woods where we can't see them."

I began to feel as if I were in the old Wild West because it was such an adventure to be riding a wild horse! The horse I was riding was caught from a wild band of horses several years ago. But, never missing a step or trying to stop, he just kept going down the trail as he called to his old wild friends. What a sweet horse!

He was a good sized horse at 15 hands (4" for each hand) or more and I noticed that on some of the trees, at about my head level, there were big scratch marks. I asked our faithful leader about the big scratch marks and John said, "You probably don't want to know!" But, curiosity got the best of me and I insisted that he tell all.

So he said, "those marks are from the grizzly bear's claw marks as they scratch the trees to sharpen them." I was very quiet for a while. Then I asked, "Do you think we'll see a bear?" John said it was not likely because we were too noisy with all the horses and pack animals. Besides, we were talking and laughing, too. Then he reassured me that his big rifle was with him. Little did I know that even a big rifle does not always stop a grizzly bear. What you don't know sometimes, can't hurt you. At least you hope so!

We left the tree line and followed the trail as it wound its way up the 7,000 ft. mountain pass, around big boulders, finally cresting the top. The view was like the eagles must see, because it went as far as your eyes could see! It was almost more than your eyes could take in – full of beauty beyond any description. We rode down the other side of the mountain into a gorgeous valley untouched by man. John said he had not been back here for many years and few people knew about the trail.

We rode down the valley for several miles and came to some thick woods. That's when we first began to hear a distant howl. Then we heard another howl from the other side of the valley. After riding a little farther, we heard another howl from up the trail. This kept happening as we rode deeper into the valley. John said it was the wolves and they were announcing that someone was coming into their valley. It was a spine chilling feeling as you hear the call from one wolf to the other, knowing they were watching us, but we had no idea where they were!

The woods opened up to a lush, green valley and John said there was a good place to camp near the valley's end. Here, there was a little stream for water and a clump of trees for a camp ground.

So, we unloaded the pack horses and set up camp. I wasn't worried about the wolves. They fascinated me. But, I could still see those huge scratch marks on the tree – right by my head! We stayed in that camp site for several days and rode out each day to explore. I was the only one that was fortunate enough to actually see a wolf. He or she was big, pure white and was bounding though the woods. I only got a quick glimpse and the wolf was gone. The sounds of the calling and howling at night meant it was a good sized pack of wolves.

On the morning we were to go home, we woke up to only one horse! John had hobbled the rest of the horses so they could enjoy the lush green meadow, but, they'd all decided it was time to go home. It's a good thing John had the one horse tied so he could go after the others. He was amazed that they had traveled so far up the valley heading for home and got them just in time - before they started over the pass. You see, God has given these animals an instinct for weather changes and they knew a huge storm was coming, but we did not.

It's a good thing we packed up and headed out when we did, because when we started over the pass it began to snow and I mean snow! You could hardly see in front of you because it was coming down so thick and fast. When we got over the pass and headed down the mountain, John said that if we'd waited another hour, we wouldn't have made it over the pass. I'm so glad the horses warned us and we didn't stay another day.

Later, my husband went back to the property that we were looking at in the middle of winter and the weather was harsh. I forgot to tell you there is no electricity in that valley. And, the closest big grocery store (for buying supplies) is three hours away and the roads are not good.

While my husband was walking he stumbled in the snow and fell. Our dog came running over to see what was wrong. Right then as he was pulling his face from the snow, he decided that this weather was just too harsh for me, and he was right! Thank God he realized that before we sold everything and moved up there. It's fun to visit but not my cup of tea for everyday living. I love the mountains and the wilderness, but I love my conveniences, too!

CHAPTER 7

"Stars First Baby"

Mark 10:27 "....with men it is impossible but not with God, for with God all things are possible."

As usual, I was sleeping in the barn to be there for Star. She is such a kind sweet mare that I know she will be a good mom. That night she was beginning to sweat and pace, so I knew things were getting close. I try to stay out of the way and let the mares be alone as much as possible when they give birth. She seemed to know that and would come over and look at me over the stall and then get back to pacing. I was beginning to get worried because she seemed to be so uncomfortable and up and down, up and down and sweating. Finally after what seemed like hours and hours she lay down hard and began to push. It was early that morning after a very long night of labor, that she had a beautiful dark bay colt with a big, wide blaze - almost bald face - and four white legs. He was absolutely stunning! What a relief to have such a healthy colt on the ground. I got the iodine on his navel because it was open and the iodine keeps bacteria from getting in. So you put it on several times until it closes and falls off.

Now it was time to go by the clock. He must move those long legs and get up to eat in at least two hours in order to not miss the colostrum in the mare's first milk. The colt did great and got up. He struggled around, learning how to use those very long legs, then he must find out where breakfast is served (I have had foals that found everything, including the stall wall, but could not find the mare's udder). However, this little guy was really smart and seemed to know just where to go. Star was a little sore from being so full of milk and she was not sure she wanted this little brown thing bumping her with his nose. But in time, all went well. He had his first milk and then took a nap to rest until the next time he would use those big, long legs to get up and eat (which happens about every 20 minutes or so). The next thing I was watching for when he got up was if his plumbing worked. It is important that the new foal "pops a cork" - at least that's what we breeders call it. A cork is a dark gummy substance and is first to come out so everything will work right. He was "text book perfect" and all went well. Everything was working. Now it was very critical for Star to get rid of the afterbirth. Three to four hours passed since the birth of the new colt and Star had not passed the afterbirth.

So, I called Dr. Freer and he gave her a shot to help her pass it. I continued to watch Star because if she didn't get rid of the afterbirth, it would become toxic. Even if a little piece is left in the womb it can kill a mare because its toxicity will poison the whole body of the horse. I watched and prayed for her all day and finally, after more labor, she passed the afterbirth. But it was a very long time by then - more than 12 hours. After carefully checking all of the afterbirth to make sure there were no tears or small pieces missing that could have been left in her, my heart was still not at peace. Star looked okay and the colt was eating and moving around. He seemed to be doing well. But, I had an uncomfortable feeling. I continued to watch her all evening and I couldn't resist one last check at 11:00 p.m. before I went to bed.

The next morning I got up and once again, ran to check on Star. She seemed okay and was eating and drinking but, I continued to check on her because I still had an uncomfortable feeling. It had been 36 hours since the colt was born and Star began to sweat and look very uncomfortable. Now she began rolling because she was in a full colic. I screamed at our son, Erik, to come and walk Star if he could get her up. Erik took the lead rope and got her up while I ran for the phone and called Dr. Freer. Why do these things happen after hours and late in the evening? The poor colt was frightened because his mom was thrashing about in the corral, obviously in pain. Erik tried to keep her up and walking.

Dr. Freer finally came and gave her a shot to slow the pain and settle her down - so he could check her out. Her temperature was way over 104 degrees F. It all meant that the retained afterbirth had poisoned her body and she had what is called septicemia or blood poisoning resulting from the retained placenta. The alarming part was that once symptoms develop, it is extremely difficult, if not impossible to reverse, in spite of treatment. That's according to the book "*Blessed Are the Broodmares*".

Dr. Freer did everything he could and left me with more antibiotics to give her. The antibiotics were safe for Star to take while nursing the colt. Although he didn't say anything, I didn't like the look on his face when he left. He also didn't leave me with any encouraging words.

Once again I went to God with a prayer request to save my beautiful mare, Star. I kept hearing those words I read in that book stating that once toxicity began, it's almost impossible to reverse – it means the death of the broodmare. Star was eating, but not enough to supply milk for a growing colt, so I got a bale of very special hay and introduced it slowly. She seemed to really like it, even though her appetite was not normal. Each day was a struggle to get her to eat enough, but finally her temperature came down to 102 degrees F and we all felt better. The septicemia poisoning had not taken my precious Star.

We passed the critical point and **God had once again answered my prayer**! We experienced miracle #3 in the life of this very special mare. But there are more miracles to come in the life of this pretty Arab mare.

CHAPTER 8

"Never Again"

Psalms 34:7 "The righteous cry out and the Lord hears and delivers them out of their trouble."

A year passed and I decided to breed Star again to Cisco. This time I was really hoping for a pinto baby. Cisco, my stallion, is a chestnut and white pinto, so there would be a 50/50 chance of getting a pinto. Once again I slept in the barn and waited each night for something to happen. We had waited for 345 days for Star to give birth, which is still normal for a horse. That morning I saw that Star was sweating and in labor. So I stayed right with her and didn't leave for any reason. It hadn't been very long, but I felt extremely uncomfortable. I just sensed a feeling of distress in me. So, I asked our son, Erik, to watch Star once again while I went to call Dr. Freer. The doctor came immediately. My guess was that he heard the panic in my voice, even though it wasn't that the labor was long, but the fact that I just didn't feel right.

Upon his arrival, Dr. Freer did an internal exam. One look at his face and I could see we were in real trouble. He said the foal's head and neck were deflected to one side and blocking the birth canal. In the book *"Blessed are the Brood Mares"* the author says that *"this is a malposition not commonly encountered and is very serious - usually you lose both mare and foal. The foal's forelegs appear straight and somewhat ready but nothing can happen. The head and neck are turned onto its side and tightly squeezed backward against its rib cage, causing a complete blockage. A foal in this position results in both the foal and mare's death, unless, professional help that is familiar with this serious problem, are there immediately."*

Dr. Freer got right to work and began trying to turn the foal inside of Star. Time and time again Dr. Freer tried in vain to turn the foal. When he turned the head and tried to pull its front feet, the foal turned its head back. We were running out of time. Again, I prayed for a miracle. Now, the doc had our son hold the foal's front feet and try to keep them in position. Dr. Freer went in again and turned the foal's head as Erik pulled on the feet and I prayed.

Believe it or not, we did this several times and praise God, it finally worked! We saw the nose of the foal as it came out in Dr. Freer's arms, because Star was standing up. Miracle #4 was a beautiful bay and white pinto colt and Star was still alive!

When it was all over, Dr. Freer turned to me and said, "Either I'm getting old or that was one of the hardest deliveries I've ever had!" It took 45 minutes, which is also a miracle, because that's a long time for a foal to be in that position and not delivered. Remember that a foal in that position usually results in the death of both mare and foal. I was so thankful that it was all over and I truly thanked God for another miracle for my beautiful bay, Arab mare, Star. So, I made a vow that I would never breed her again! She is far too special to go through any of that.

CHAPTER 9

"Another Move – God's Timing!"

Rev. 3:7 "He who is Holy. He who is true. He who has the keys of David. He who opens doors that no one shuts and shuts doors that no one opens."

We had lived in this beautiful beach home for over 12 years, but my husband and I both felt like God was moving us on. We began looking all over the state and finally decided that Whatcom County was where we wanted to settle. We were attending a church in Bellingham at the time. So we listed our very special low- bank sandy, beach front home with a large real estate agency. We found a real nice 18-acre ranch in Bellingham and it was on a Friday that we made an offer with a contingency that we must sell our beach home. On Saturday, a doctor made a cash offer on the ranch and we lost out. We were both very disappointed, but later down the road, we were thanking God that He closed that door. We continued to look at property, but finally gave up and decided to wait until our beach home was sold. Then we could make a good offer.

Our beach home did not sell for three years. The real estate people said we were not over priced, so that was not the reason. We just had to find the right person. That September I got tired of the "looky-loos", so we took it off the market. It was then that we took the signs down. The thought of a rest from all the people trudging through our home was nice, so, we decided to take the winter off and start again with the realtors the following summer.

In February, someone told me about a place I should go and see. I called the real estate lady who had it listed and she showed me a 5-acre farm. It was ugly, yet it had a view, but not great. She asked me what I was looking for and I said, "My husband likes the mountains with a really good view and I raise horses." She said, "Then you must go look at my boss's ranch which is for sale!" I asked her how much they wanted. After telling me the price, I gulped and told her it was out of our price range. She was like a Joshua and insisted that I go look at the ranch. So, I went to look at the ranch and I fell in love!

As I walked in the 2-year-old house, it opened up to a view of Mt. Baker and the mountain looked like a big ice cream cone! The ranch had 40 acres, a beautiful house and had been fenced for buffalo. There were no horse barns, but it had a big old milking barn for cows. I brought my husband and he loved it too. We prayed and brought friends to look at the house and the property. Then, we prayed and blessed the land. One of the elderly men that came with us is prophetic and my husband asked him, "Well, Dave, what is God saying to you?" Dave took some time, and then looked at both of us, "You will know if this is God, if your house on the island sells."

That was not the answer we were looking for. Or house had not sold in three years and now it was not even on the market! Dave told us that on a Saturday and we both went away feeling a little discouraged and wondering what we should do. That Monday afternoon a man walked up the beach and knocked on our door and said that he was told our place was 'for sale' several months prior to that and he wondered if we were still interested in selling our home? The man had been walking on the beach earlier and asked a neighbor if she knew of any homes for sale that were on the beach. That same man paid us CASH for our beach home! The people with the 40-acre ranch came down in price and we were able to buy that ranch. We even had enough money to build a very nice 6-stall horse barn with a tack room and foaling stall (for birthing horses). God has a plan and it's always a good plan!

CHAPTER 10

"Lost at Night"

Psalms 139:12 "Indeed, the darkness shall not hide from You, but the night shines as the day; the darkness and the light are both alike to You."

The kind of mountain riding I really love is with a bunch of friends. We all save a week each summer to get together and camp at Brice Creek Campground in the Cascade Mountains. It has horse corrals and water for the critters.

Most of us are grandmothers or close to being grandparents. So, we can relax and have fun, take a morning ride, come back and eat lunch, then take a nap or play board games. We can do what we like, maybe ride again or just relax. The one thing that almost always happens is lots of laughter and singing!

One summer, Seattle was hit with record heat and it was nearly 100 degrees the week we were at Brice Creek. It was too hot to ride during the day, so we just sat in lawn chairs and sprayed water on ourselves. We tried riding in the late afternoon, and almost got eaten alive by the mosquitoes! My poor horse, Cisco, was covered with bites. So we decided to ride a little later.

Did I mention that there were a couple of blondes in the group? Including me! The next night we saddled up at about 7:30 p.m. and got going about 8:00 p.m. Well, off we went for an evening ride. We were laughing, singing and having a wonderful time when someone noticed it was getting dark. One of the blondes was leading, perhaps it was me, and we turned around to go back to camp.

When we came to the first intersecting trail, no one could remember which trail we had taken! There are so many trails and switchbacks, trails crossing trails, that it's very easy to get lost. None of us had a clue which way to go. I was in the lead and simply made a decision to go back in the direction that I thought would head to camp. At the next trail intersection, I let someone else make the choice and off we all went. We were still singing, but I think it was more like the Lord's prayer - that He lead us by still waters and get us back to camp!

By now, I was beginning to think we were just going in circles and we probably were. None of us had a flashlight and it was beginning to get very dark. We thought that maybe we should just give the horses their heads (sometimes it works to ride with a very loose rein and let your horse make the decision) and let them lead us home. That was probably a good idea, but we continued to go in the direction we thought the camp would be. All of us were very confused as to the direction and there were no stars – it was very dark in the forest. I forgot to mention that there are also bears and cougars in this area. That subject was brought up, but we quickly went on to something else, because no one wanted to think about wild animals! We just wanted to get safely back to camp. Continuing to pick our way carefully down the trail in the darkness, all of a sudden, the trail came out on the main road that enters the camp on the opposite side from where we rode out earlier!

How on earth we got clear on the other side of the campground, none of us could figure out, but we rejoiced because we could simply ride the road back to camp in the middle of a very dark night. What an experience that was! To this day, none of us can figure out how we got on the main road back to camp when we began our ride in the opposite direction. It must have been God!

CHAPTER 11

"Glimpse Into Heaven"

Revelation 19:11 "Now I saw heavens opened and behold - a white horse. And He who sat on him was called Faithful and true."

Remember the bay and white filly that I got with the big head, long legs and beautiful, blue eyes named Mayim? She turned out to be one of the most incredible horses I ever had in over 50 years of owning horses. She grew into her head and legs and was absolutely elegant!

Mayim had a long, thick, white mane that went down past her shoulders to her front legs and a big, long, flowing white tail. I could put anybody on her and she would take care of them. She always came in first or second at the Fox Trotter shows. When we showed at the gaited horse shows, she would get a First Place or at least a Second Place. An amazing mare, Mayim loved people and being with them. She loved to go on the trail and people would stop me whenever I rode her on them. They would always comment about how gorgeous she was with her beautiful, flowing, mane and tail. But, most of all, I loved this mare because she was just so special, beautiful and very kind.

As I was getting ready to teach a class at church one morning, I got a call on my cell phone to come home because there was a problem with the horses. So I came home in a rush and found the horses had gotten into the hay barn. All of them came out except Mayim. She had stepped into a pallet board with her back leg and hoof and when she went to go out the door the pallet stuck in the door. As Mayim was trying to get out of the board, she fell over and broke her back leg. When I found her, she was standing with her back leg up. We called the vet, who came immediately and took x-rays, wrapped her leg in a temporary cast, then left to develop the pictures.

By this time, my friend Karen Whitmen was at my side. Before the vet left he said it did not look too good. My head was spinning and my heart was pounding. How could this happen? This was my best horse and I loved her so much.

The vet called back after reading the x-rays and suggested that I load Mayim in the trailer and bring her to the Kulshan Veterinary Hospital. As usual, she was so willing to please and hopped right in the trailer on three legs! When my husband, Karen, and I got to the clinic, three vets had already looked at the x-rays. They had also consulted with Pilchuck, a veterinary hospital not too far away in Snohomish, which specialized in surgery and the broken legs of horses. All the veterinarians agreed that even if Mayim had surgery she would always be in pain because the broken leg was so bad, it could not be completely repaired. The thought of this beautiful mare living in pain all of her life was horrifying to me - so I helplessly agreed that the best thing to do was to put her down. I felt like I was in a night mare and would wake up soon, because this really could not be happening to me! How could this happen to my beautiful Mayim? Mayim was the mare whose name even means *living* water.

I've watched this procedure many times in my years of owning horses and had horses put down for all kinds of reasons, mostly old age. It's never nice to witness, but it can definitely be an act of kindness. The vet gives the horse a shot in their vein and they drop their head and just fall over dead. Not so with Mayim! The vet gave her the shot and her head went up in the air, her ears pricked up and her eyes were looking far up into the sky. It really looked like she saw something.

Then it was over, and my beautiful Mayim fell to the ground. The shock of her death hit me and I cried. I wept for my beautiful Mayim because she was gone. Later, when Karen and I talked about this we both agreed that God gave Mayim a look into heaven and she saw the great white horse that is talked about in *Revelation 19:11*. Actually, God did that for me, because now I know that there are horses in heaven with the great white horse. I know that my Mayim is in heaven roaming the green fields and she will be there when I go home to Jesus. Even in this tragedy, God gave me something good. He gave me such hope in eternal life. He opened up heaven for a horse to see what is up there and in doing that - He gave me new hope!

CHAPTER 12

"Nutmeg's Choice"

James 1:17 *"Every good and perfect gift comes from above."*

Another miracle came out of this tragedy. By this time I had been breeding horses for an easy 30 years. With mares it's hormonal and when they come into a "heat" cycle once a month, it's right then they are ready to breed and they don't usually care who it is doing the breeding! I have a very well-bred Fox Trotter mare and is she ever wild! You can't look at her or touch her. Her name is Nutmeg. She was purchased at an auction in Wyoming because of her great blood lines by the breeder where I at first got all my Fox Trotters. Apparently, she was drugged at the auction. When Joan got her home to Washington, she had a different, untouchable horse.

But, Nutmeg had incredible babies. Now, Joan is one of the best horse trainers I have ever been around and I used her to put 30 days on all my young horses. But, even Joan said to not try any round pen work with Nutmeg because she will die before giving in. The friend that I got Nutmeg from built a chute to run Nutmeg into for trimming her feet and administering shots. That was the only way to expedite any vetting or trimming. First, the vet would give Nutmeg a sedative to quiet her so the farrier could trim her hooves and the vet could give her vaccines. Not having a chute to run horses into, I wasn't sure what I was going to do with Nutmeg. I tried everything with Nutmeg when I first got her. I would simply sit in her stall every day to make her come up to me while I held her grain in a pan and made her eat by me. I did this for months and nothing changed with Nutmeg. If I would move or look at her she would fly to the other side of the stall and snort and snort. She would eat her food and when done, she would go to the far side of the stall. When I got up she would snort and panic. I always spoke to her very low and soft and moved slow but she did not want anything to do with humans - except to get her food.

But, Nutmeg has been the best broodmare I have had and the easiest horse to keep. I've had her for over ten years and have never trimmed her feet or given her a shot!

I have had many farriers look at her feet and they are amazed. The hooves always had the correct angle and wore off exactly right without any chips, cracks, or breaking. I never even had to build a chute.

I had a nasty cough go through my barn and guess who never got it? That's right – Nutmeg! She is also the healthiest horse I have ever had. Nutmeg costs me very little in hay and she requires only a small amount of grain. She is the "easiest keeper" and has produced some of my best foals. Every foal of Nutmeg's that I showed in halter classes, won top ribbons. Today, the owners of many of her babies call me to say what incredible horses they own.

You see, when Nutmeg had a foal she didn't care what you did with the foal. So, I would go in the stall and not look at Nutmeg at all - simply lower my eyes and go to the baby. But if I would turn and just look at Nutmeg, she would absolutely panic, snort and go to the far side of the foaling stall. She is still that way and I have never even raised my voice!

Now, I think she is just smart and doesn't want to be touched by anyone. Nutmeg is 25-years-old at this writing. She just enjoys being a horse out in my pasture with the other horses and doesn't want to be touched by human hands for any reason.

I have always kept Nutmeg in the pasture that was right next to my stallion, Cisco. She loved him whether she was in heat or not, so she was always easy to breed. She was so easy to breed except about six years ago! She came in "heat" and was ready to be bred, but she would have nothing to do with Cisco – this was unheard of!

Nutmeg would go to the far end of her pasture and just stand there looking across the other pastures to a far corner of my property. It was there that I had a small pen where I kept a 2 ½-year-old Fox Trotter colt called Traveler. He was out of my beautiful mare Mayim (who had broken her leg badly and had to be put to sleep).

This was a very unusual situation. I have never had a mare choose who she wanted to breed before! I guessed (at the time) that Nutmeg simply wanted a younger man.

I moved Cisco so he could not see this "unheard of relationship" between Nutmeg and the young stallion. I determined that his feelings would not be hurt if he couldn't see Nutmeg and Traveler.

The breeding between Nutmeg and Traveler was an absolute miracle because they produced a clone of my mare Mayim! This filly I named "Mirror Image" because she looks exactly like Mayim though we call her Emily. She has the same big, blue eyes with bay and white markings in almost the same places as Mayim. She even looks at me the same way her grandmother, Mayim, would look at me. It's almost eerie. I have put my arms around Emily and just cried because she is such a gift from God. She has replaced my loss and heartbreak with Mayim and I am so grateful! *Romans 8:28* says that all things work together for good to those who love God. If Nutmeg hadn't chosen the younger stallion, I would have never bred him to her and I would have missed a very special gift from God!

Star

Star 3 Years old

Rosemary in in official Miss Spokane First Nations Regalia

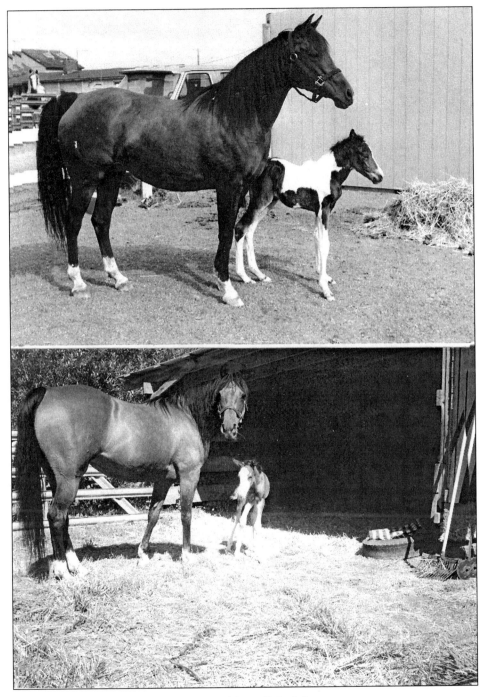

Star and her 2 babies

Harness family sisters Judy and Jeany , brother Bill and baby Rosemary

Mountain we rode over to the Valley of the wolves in BC Canada

Rosemary age 14 on River

Wild mare, Nutmeg

Top picture Rosemary and Emily, Mirror Image of Mayim

Bottom picture Rosemary and Mayim

Cicso my stallion and me

Amie a gift from God

WITEZ II

The fascinating story of the great Arabian, Witez II, begins in
Poland where he was foaled in 1938. It was the Poles who reared
him and the Germans who cared for him as he endured the
hardships of the second world war. In 1945 Patton's 3rd Army
finally rescued this gallant stallion and brought him to the United
States. Here Witez II achieved his greatest fame by founding a
dynasty of beautiful Arabians to rival that of Man O' War. This
horse (whose name meant chieftan and knight, prince and hero)
surely fulfilled the promise of his title.

Witez II

CHAPTER 13

"Emily – Mirror Image"

Psalms 37:4 "Delight thyself also in the LORD and He shall give you the desires of your heart."

When Emily was first born her front legs were so knocked-kneed and crooked she could hardly walk. I had my veterinarian, Dr. Sauter, from Kulshan Veterinary Hospital, come to look at Emily. Dr. Sauter has worked with a lot of thoroughbreds from the racetrack and really understood leg problems. He examined Emily very carefully the very first day she was born. He said he had seen many thoroughbreds born with legs like this (even worse) and they will usually straighten out with time. It was also important to get her trimmed regularly and properly. So that is exactly what we did. I took pictures of her to see the very slow improvement. In all my years of raising horses I had never seen a horse as knocked-kneed as Emily. It looked really scary to me! But as time went on, she grew into those very long and knock-kneed legs and began to get stronger. Her legs began to very slowly straighten out.

When she was 1 ½ years old my farrier commented on her left knee that looked a little swollen. Emily's knees were both different and funny in shape because she had been so crooked. But it did look like that one knee was a little puffy in front. So I decided the vet should take a look. Dr. Sauter took an x-ray and sure enough there was a bone chip floating around in her knee. How could this be, because she wasn't even even lame or favoring that leg? The doctor stated that she would need surgery but the surgery should not be done until the knee bones were closed.

The knees usually close after a horse is two years old or so. So, Dr. Sauter sent Emily's x-ray to Pilchuck Veterinary Hospital in Snohomish. As I said before, they specialize in bone surgery for horses. So the decision was made to have Emily checked after she was two years old and if the knee bones were closed, we would do the surgery.

The next summer Emily had an appointment to see if her knees were closed and she was ready for surgery. My friend Karen once again was with me. Her daughter Katherine lives right in Snohomish so we decided to stay there. We brought Emily and checked her into the hospital the day before the surgery. The actual surgery only took about an hour that next morning. I waited at Katherine's (Karen's daughter) home for a call all day. I felt like I was on pins and needles. No one called me all day.

Finally at 5:00 pm I called the hospital and they had been so busy they did not have time to call and let me know that everything had gone just fine. And, Emily should be a sound horse after her recovery. She stayed in the hospital for another day so they could check her carefully and make sure everything was okay.

The next morning we went in for a consultation with the surgeon so he could explain how to take care of Emily at home. She had a huge bandage that went from the top of her leg to the bottom - the size of a huge cast. Because recovery of the surgery would be quite painful, she wouldn't be able to put weight on that leg. So, they wrapped the other front leg. I looked at that and could not figure out how she was going to bend her leg and step up into the horse trailer. The bandages were like a full leg cast and they wouldn't bend. But, Emily is like her grandmother, Mayim, and she is willing to be obedient. She just looked at the horse trailer and hopped with both feet up and her front end went right into the trailer!

The vet's instructions for Emily were that she was to be confined in a stall for one month. She has never been confined in a stall except here at the hospital. Following that first month of confinement, she could be hand walked 2-3 times a day on short walks for another month. The third month she would be able to be in a small turn-out during the day and continue the hand led walks. Emily is a very quiet, sweet-natured horse, but, having never been locked in a stall, she was not a happy camper. After a week or so I had to remove the huge bandage and cast to make sure it was okay underneath and replace it with new wrap. Here I was once again becoming a veterinarian!

The bandage had rubbed the back of her knee and it was now raw, so I called the veterinarian and he said to cut a hole in the thick, cotton matting and the raw skin would not be touched by the rest of the wrap. He also told me to put some anti-bacterial ointment on the raw skin. And we still had to put a leg wrap on her good leg to give it support.

I thought my walks with Emily would be nice, casual, pleasant walks, but Emily had other ideas! She was two years old and wanted to run and play, which was defiantly against the doctor's orders. Those times were a real work out for me because I had to keep her at a walk. Again, it took a long time but that summer Emily was fully recovered. I did not work her at all that year, but I did, indeed, turn her out that fall to play and just be a horse!

I didn't begin any training with her until the next fall, when she was three years old. I started at the end of September and had a few rides on her before winter came and Emily's training came to a close. Emily is a beautiful 4-year-old mare now and I have started training her again. She has an absolute 'smooth as glass' fox-trot and just like her grandmother she loves to please! At this time I have only ridden her out in the pasture, but I think she is going to be a wonderful riding horse.

CHAPTER 14

"Police Training"

Matthew 6:8 "For your Heavenly Father knows the things you have need of before you ask Him."

N ow, I had graduated from riding Emily in the round-pen to riding her in the small pasture in front of our house, though each ride was only about 15-20 minutes. I had been on her back about 20 times when I decided to enroll Emily and myself in a Police Class being held at a stable near here. I called and asked if I could bring a green (unexperienced) horse to the class. They said yes. So, on the first day of class I loaded Emily in my trailer and off we went! Remember Emily has never been ridden off the property, let alone with other horses in an indoor arena. I took her out of the trailer and her head shot straight up and her big, blue eyes almost bugged out of her head. I thought to myself, "Oh no, this does not look good. I could be in for the ride of my life!" The first hour or so was basically instructions for the rider, so we were able to put our horses in a stall while we went to class. When it was time to ride I went to get Emily and she was back to her quiet self. She is amazing!

The instructor wanted a volunteer for the round pen part so I volunteered Emily, and explained that she was very "green". After a few minutes of work with Emily the instructor said I needed another horse. "This one is too compliant." Yea, for Emily!

Now the real test would come because it was time to saddle up and mount each horse in the arena. It was all new for Emily. She stood very still and was very quiet while I got on because that's one thing that's really important to someone my age. I always got on her and then would just sit for 2-3 minutes so she would learn to stand quietly when I mounted. Other horses were moving about and warming up and Emily just stood still. Bless her heart. Before we started any obstacles, the instructor would have us do a police drill. That was to get the horses a little tired so they would not be so spooky. Most of the drill was done at good trot. That was great for me because Emily doing her fox trot is smooth as silk and so we just glided by while others were frantically posting up and down in the saddle. Even the instructor commented about how easy Emily made it look because she was so smooth.

The obstacles started out on the ground, over poles and across big, plastic tarps. That was a hard one for most of the horses - except Emily. So the instructor would say, "Bring that little pinto up and have her go in front of the other horses so they will follow her." This was the 'green' horse leading the well trained other horses. I could not believe it!

From the ground we went to going through tarps that were hanging down and cut in strips. We had to ride through them. To a horse this looks like a solid wall but they are amazing animals but, usually they obey their rider even when asked to go through a wall! Well, some of the horses did and others just plain refused to do what their riders asked of them. Then, we had to get used to going through areas where things would touch them on both sides and could be moving at the same time. Also, loud noises, sirens, police car lights going and balls thrown at the horse and bouncing by. Flames were shooting up 3-4 feet from big flares where we had to go in and out of the flames.

We practiced crowd control by following right next to a moving car with the siren blaring! All this was accomplished in 20 hours. Both Emily and I have framed certificates of our 20 hours of Police class that we both passed.

I think everyone was just as amazed as I was at how Emily simply handled it all. You see God knew I needed a horse that would not be spooky and would trust me to keep her safe no matter how scary things looked and sounded. I feel so blessed to have this little horse.

Emily is a mirror image of Mayim, but a smaller version and maybe even quieter!

CHAPTER 15

"Entertaining Angels Unaware"

Hebrews 13:2 "Do not forget to entertain strangers, for by so doing some have unwittingly entertained angels."

Anytime you choose to love there is always the risk of being hurt. But, the love far outweighs the risk. To never have loved is to never have lived.

People have always asked when I first got the love of horses. If my mom were alive, she would tell you that I was born with it! She said that from the time I was 2-years-old until the age of five or six, I would gallop across our house on my knees, whinnying and clicking like I had horse's hooves. My mom said I actually wore the rug out! When I wasn't galloping in the house, I was playing out side with a stick horse and I mean STICK. It didn't have a fancy head like a kid's stick horse has on it today. It was a real stick, because that's all I had!

My neighborhood friends and I would play for hours with popsicle sticks and rocks and mud making huge horse farms with roads and little villas. All of these horse farms were made with whatever we could find. We created and invented things for our farms with our own hand-made toys. At this time we had no television set, so the whole outdoors was ours to explore! The TV didn't tell us what our toys should look like, so we created them with our own imaginations.

My Dad was a pastor of mostly very small country churches. Have you ever heard the expression "poorer then a church mouse"? It was my older sister that told me, when I was older, that we were very poor. I never knew I was poor. How could you be poor when all you can remember is enjoying and playing endlessly your friends? I also remember that we were loved uncondi- tionally by our parents. I am sure I must have worn old hand me down clothes, but it didn't seem to matter to me. I didn't have any new fangled toys. I also didn't have a TV to tell me what I should be playing with and wearing so I just enjoyed life to its fullest.

I thought my Dad was a genius and he could fix anything. In our basement he had a huge wireless radio system set up and he would talk to people all over the world. He loved that kind of technology.

In fact, when I was 10 or so and the TV came about, my Dad loved it and we were the first to have a TV in our neighborhood. I can remember the whole neighborhood coming to our house and my Dad would turn on the TV. We would all sit and watch the test pattern and be amazed! Do you remember the test pattern? You know, the circles with the Indian chief's head in the middle of the screen in black and white? Amazing entertainment!

One of my Dad's favorite things to do was to explore little country roads. I loved it too because I just might see some horses out in their pastures. So, I would be like radar scanning the fields in case I would see a horse. On long trips I would fight to stay awake because I might miss seeing a big country horse enjoying his pasture.

This was great until my Dad got a new car! That means it was new to us, but definitely not a new car! This car was a disaster for me. It was an old Nash. Do you remember what they looked like? They looked like a half of a water-melon with the flat side down going along the road and little, tiny windows in the back. The seats were so deep I could not see out of the little tiny windows even if I wanted to. I hated that car.

Then, my whole life changed when I was 11. My dad was a pastor on Sunday morning, Sunday night and Wednesday night. He loved being a pastor because he loved people, but between being a pastor, he worked all kinds of jobs to make ends meet. He worked with asbestos, which today we know is very toxic and dangerous, and he was diagnosed with lung cancer. I only knew that my dad was sick, but he would soon get well. As an 11-year-old girl, no one bothered to tell me how serious it was. Even when he went to the hospital, I just knew he was going to get better and be home soon. Again, no one ever told me how serious it really was until my Mother came home from the hospital. She told me that my Dad had gone to Heaven. It came as such a shock because I had no warning. I have never cried so hard and wondered why my Dad, who loved everyone and loved life, had to die at 44 years-old?

I will never forget my Dad's funeral and the experience I had there. My Dad was friends with everyone, from the street people to the very wealthy, and they all loved him. So the overflow rooms were full and the entryway was full and had standing room only. I don't remember anything that was said at the funeral, but afterward, I remember just crying and crying. I was by myself because there were so many people. Then a very tall blond lady, dressed in a bright blue suit, (whom I thought was my aunt) came over and took me by the hand. It was this lady who led me outside, away from the crowd. Then, she sat down and held me. She hugged me and wiped my nose and I just felt so much better. She took me back inside and I don't remember much after that. The next day I told my Mom about my tall, blond aunt in the bright, blue suit, who took me outside and held me and I felt so much better. But, my Mom said "You don't have any tall, blond aunt!" I later asked my sister about the tall, blond lady in the bright, blue suit and they didn't see anyone like that even there! In fact, in those days, no one would ever wear a bright blue suit to a funeral. I believe that God sent an angel to comfort a hurting 11-year-old girl who was at the crowded funeral of her father, whom she loved.

CHAPTER 16

"River"

Psalm 91:11 "For He shall give His angles charge over you, to keep you in all your ways."

The next year my Mom married a rancher from a very small community called Hay. It was then that I got my first horse. I used to be Rosemary Harness from Hay with the horses and I loved it! My first horse's name was River. He was a golden palomino supposedly half-Arab and half-Quarter horse and he would buck and throw me off every chance he could!

I remember one time I was riding River in downtown Hay which consisted of a store, across the street from the store was a post office, maybe six or eight houses and a couple of churches. River decided to buck me off there in the middle of town, right in front of the store! River just continued to buck with his head down and his mouth open and this terrible bawling sound coming from his mouth and his eyes were closed. He bucked right into the side of the store and almost knocked himself over! He turned and continued to buck as he went down the road. I couldn't catch him until he stopped bucking and I then led him home. My step dad would get on him and ride him out in a plowed field of deep, rich, black soil till he felt the bucking was out of him. River would come home dripping wet with sweat and it would work until the next time he would buck me off. I got to be a very sensitive rider and as soon as I felt his back go up, I learned to pull River's head to my knee and he could not buck. I never could relax and ride. I had to ride and watch him every minute!

I barrel raced and stake raced him. River was as fast as lightning and no one could beat my time. The only problem was that he was very inconsistent. I would have the best time of anyone on the first day. The next day he would knock over the barrels and take all the stakes out on purpose. He definitely was a horse that had his own mind!

But, I kept River for many years. In fact, I had him until he was 20 years old. Many years later I found out that River was actually used as a practice, bucking horse for some rodeo guys. They never told my step-dad that little fact! Who, in their right mind, would sell a bucking horse to a 12-year-old to ride? I never had any lessons on horses, but I think I learned a lot just from staying on River and "listening" to his body language. I learned to never let anyone but my step-dad ride River because he always threw everyone else off!

I went to Whitworth College in Spokane, Washington and I bought an English saddle from one of the girls in my dorm. I did not have a clue what

I was doing, but I wanted to jump. So I went home, put up some poles and I would jump River over them. He was good and I could feel his body even better with this tiny, postage-stamp, English saddle than I ever did with my bigger, western saddle. I set-up the jumps in a field just down the road from my house because it was a flat field. After jumping the 2 foot-high poles, I was riding home and forgot to pay attention. Not a good thing to do on River because he just jumped up in the air and came down into a hard buck without a single warning! You see, I had been away at school and River had not been ridden for many months, so I went flying over his head and belly-flopped right on the hard road like a pancake! The wind was knocked out of me, so I didn't get up for a while. River quit bucking and just stood there surprised because it had been years since he had bucked me off. I finally got up and got back on and rode him home. That night I had a date with a good friend and with a very sore body, but I went anyway. The next morning I was really hurting internally. So, my mom took me to the doctor and the doctor put me in the hospital because he said I had bruised my spleen. I was Miss Spokane at the time and the *Spokesmen Review* newspaper published an article with the headline: "*Postage stamp saddle puts Miss Spokane in the hospital.*" That reporter didn't know about River! I recovered and was out of the hospital in a few days.

CHAPTER 17

"A Dog's Life"

Psalm 139:17-18 "How precious are Your thoughts to me, Oh God. How great is the sum of them. If I should count them, they would be more in number than the sand."

Some of you are probably wondering if God only cares for my horses. Well, if you remember the story of "Noah and the Ark", God saved all the animals two by two. *Matthew 10:29* says that God knows when even a sparrow falls to the ground. It also goes on to say that God knows every hair on our head. I have a lot of hair so that says a lot, and though some of you may not have so much hair, he loves you just like you are!

I've had Dalmatians since 1974. They are known to be the "coach" dogs and ran with the horse wagons – including the first fire-wagons pulled by horses. I got my first Dalmation while I was living on the east coast. Her name was Pebbles, and she was wild, and I mean wild! The veterinarian said to let her have a litter of pups and that would settle her down, but he was wrong, because she was still wild. Then he said to have her fixed. So we did, and she was still wild. She just would almost bounce off the walls. If she ever got out of our fence she was gone! We would chase her and she would just run, but she always came home the next day or so. Actually, I ended up giving her to some relatives who lived on a farm. Pebbles was just fine at the farm because she loved being out side and running around free. I was living in town at the time so it worked out well for all of us.

I never had another "wild" Dalmatian again. Dalmations have lots of energy and love to go for walks, and especially horseback rides. But they also love people and love to be with you.

Espresso was a dog I owned years ago and he definitely had his own personality - he growled all the time because he was actually talking, but it did sound a little scary!

I bought him with money I made when I took an Espresso Bar down to Quartzite, Arizona. At that time, Quartzite had the world's biggest flea market and gem/rock show. The population would swell to a million people passing through the town. The people were mostly snowbirds, or rather, folks who wintered in Arizona. My husband was going to help his friend with some electrical work for about a month at what was called "The Mane Event", which consisted of hundreds of booths with stuff for sale from everywhere. That's why I decided to take an Espresso Bar down there and make some money!

This was in the early 1980's and Espresso Bars were becoming very popular in Seattle, but remained little known in most other places.

So, I got a booth and decorated it and put all my bottles of flavor lined up so people could see what a wonderful choice they would have. You know, like Crème d'Menthe, Pina Colada, and Amaretto. You would not believe the looks of horror when elderly snowbirds would walk by, thinking I was selling alcohol! I would try and convince them that it was only flavors for coffee. They couldn't believe anyone would pay $1.50 (at that time!) for a 12-oz cup of coffee!

But, there were many truckers and people from Seattle who would see my sign and stop just to get a good cup of coffee. They were surprised to see an Espresso Bar out in the desert of Arizona. Today, espresso stands are popular all across America and nearly every gas station, store and corner has a drive-through espresso stand. I was a pioneer for the coffee world in the desert. And with the money I earned, I purchased my next Dalmation, and named him Espresso.

My dog, Espresso, lived a very long, good life. But, when he was almost 13-years-old, his arthritis got so bad he couldn't get up anymore. I had the terrible decision of putting him to sleep. I hated those times, but knew it was best for my loving dog. My vet was so good because when I brought Espresso to the clinic, he came out and put Espresso to sleep in the back of my station wagon. I was sobbing because it was so hard to lose a pet that you loved so much. We then took him home and buried him between two fir trees in our lane.

I don't do well without a dog to love, so I began looking for Dalmatian in the paper and everywhere, but there were none. I was always looking.

Then our son, Ryan, saw one on the internet at a rescue place. I called and talked to the *Colville Rescue Center* and they explained that the 3-year-old dog was found in a kennel. He was extremely thin because he'd had no food or water for days and the dog was in very poor condition. I decided to come and look at him. We drove across the state and stayed with our son, Shay, his wife Katie and 2- year-old-daughter, Shaelynn, who lived in Spokane. It was always a treat to visit the grandchildren!

Later, we drove up north to look at the dog. Thin was not the word! You could see every bone in this little dog's body. I have never seen anything like it. My heart was broken. We let him out of the kennel where the rescue volunteer had been keeping him and he was so weak and poorly coordinated that he could hardly walk. I think my husband thought I was crazy, but I just could not leave that little dog with out seeing if I could help him! So, we took him home. The volunteers named this dog Trooper because he was trying so hard to survive.

I got Trooper home and fixed up a box stall in my horse barn with a run out side. I worked with my vet for about six months and finally, we were able to put some weight on him! During that time I made special food for him, a mixture of brown rice and cooked hamburger. But, Trooper kept getting sick with infections and fevers.

My daughter, Tiffany is married to a veterinarian, Dr. Terry Beatty, so he graciously examined the dog at my house when they came for a visit. He said this dog had a specific disease. It was a very, very long medical term. Terry took me to the internet and showed me examples of other dogs with this problem. Their insides are all mixed up with their outside organs and they continually have infections and health problems. Terry said surgery was possible by a specialist but, there is only a 50/50 chance of success and the surgery would probably cost up to $5000. So I was faced again with putting another dog to sleep. I was a mess after this one and was very disappointed. I just didn't have the heart to even look for another dog, yet, my heart was longing for another Dalmatian.

Time passed and I was walking down to the hay barn to take care of the horses. I was talking to God and said out of my mouth "God, if you want me to have another Dalmatian, you'll just have to bring one here to my house". That was the end of my prayer and I simply went to the horses without another thought.

The next week I got a call from the *Colville Pet Rescue*. They had another Dalmatian for me, having bought her out of the classifieds because she is a registered dog and they were afraid that a puppy mill would buy her. A puppy mill is where they have many dogs and all the dogs do is produce as many puppies as possible so their owners can sell them. The poor dog's living conditions are usually not good (a tiny cage) because all the people care about is getting puppies to sell. The lady also added, "We have a volunteer who is willing to drive her over to your house". Can you believe that I just prayed asking God to bring a Dalmatian to my house and here He is already answering my prayer? So, you see, God cares about all of our animals. If it's important to us, it's important to God. He is interested in everything in our lives.

When the lady called to get directions to our home I thought it would be nice for her to meet us halfway, in Ellensburg. Because, if the lady drove over here, the round trip drive would have been twelve or fourteen hours, depending which way she drove. We love going to the Cowboy Church in Ellensburg and so we would just meet her at the Cowboy church. We met, and I got Amie who is the most wonderful Dalmatian. She is the best dog I have ever had! But what do you expect when it's God Who brings you a dog?

CHAPTER 18

"Ice Scare"

Joshua 1:9 "Be strong and of good courage, do not be afraid, nor be dismayed, for the Lord your God is with you wherever you go."

As many of you know, horses are very expensive. If you did not know that, let me tell you that they are very expensive to keep, not just to buy. I had many horses given to me for free, but it's feeding and taking care of their feet and keeping them healthy (vet bills) that's expensive. So, I decided to support my "horse habit" by boarding horses. Having 40 acres of beautiful grass and trees and 14 stalls for horses with pens and runs, it made perfect sense.

My family and I have met some wonderful people by boarding their horses and we all became very good friends. While some horses have very unique personalities and are quite interesting, we have also had some horses do pretty crazy things, too!

Twice, I have had a horse go through the ice into the freezing water below. One horse that belongs to Julie (a boarder at my place), did just that. The horse's name is Glory. Glory is a big, brown Tennessee Walking horse. She is a very funny horse, with big, huge ears and a big head - because she is a big horse! She also has two big, sad, brown eyes that just pull a person into her and make you wonder what might be done to make her happier. Glory is the kind of horse that you just want to love and make her happy. She is a very sweet mare, but a little independent. She kind of just did her own thing, even in the herd, and was often by herself in her own world.

Now, we live in the direct path of harsh northeastern winds. They come down from Frazier Canyon in B.C. during the winter and can be horrible! Perhaps only five inches of snow fall but the winds will blow them into five-foot drifts of snow!

That is exactly what happened. We were having a northeastern storm and had snowfall of about six inches deep with 15 degrees F temperatures. With the "wind chill factor" you're looking at probably -10 degrees F or less. That's cold for this part of the country (Ferndale, WA). I noticed that the P.U.D. (public utilities) had a big tractor plowing the road that goes to the river because the snowdrifts were so high their trucks could not make it down to check the pump station on the river. P.U.D. has never done that before because the storms do not usually last too many days and the drifts will melt before they need to check the station.

I looked out my dining room window past the five acre pasture in front of the house to the 20-acre pasture. Both pastures had huge patches of green where the wind had blown the snow off. Because we are not too far from a river we have drainage ditches across some of our fields. These ditches, in the winter, can be full of water. It was then that I just happened to see the top of a horse's head popping up. Because we already had another horse go through the ice I knew exactly what was going on, because this horse was in almost the same place!

Earlier we had some flooding and there was a lot of water over the ditches, so I went out there while my husband ran to get the tractor. My daughter-in-law, Brandy, just happened to be here and we both ran to see which horse it was. There was another friend here who picked up a big tow line that was used for cars. Grabbing a halter and some ropes, off we went while the wind bit at our faces. When we got closer, and I saw those big ears and big, sad eyes that now had a panicked look in them. It was Glory. She had wondered away from the herd and the snow drifts had totally covered the ditch so that you could not even see that there was a ditch there anymore! She had broken through the ice and was in the icy water up to her neck.

I didn't think about it at the time, but everything just fell into place. My daughter-in-law, Brandy, is tall and very thin and couldn't weigh 100 pounds soaking wet. She was visiting and the only one weighing in so scantly that she could get out on the ice close enough to put the tow rope around Glory. Then,

I knew that hypothermia was setting in because Glory quit struggling and simply closed her eyes as if she were going to sleep. You see, I didn't know just how long she was in that water, while her whole body was submerged in freezing water with the wind blowing in her face – and it was freezing too!

I got as close as I dared on the ice. When she would drift off, I'd take the rope and hit her in the face to keep her awake and I'd follow it up by yelling at her. Maybe it sounds cruel but it probably helped save her life.

Brandy was able to get the tow rope under one leg and across the other side and over her neck. How she did this I am really not sure – it had to be a miracle.

But where was my husband, Ragnar, with the tractor? Glory was slipping fast and it was taking a lot more screaming and hitting her to keep her awake! In the meantime, Ragnar had gotten completely stuck in a five-foot snow drift trying to get to the horse. He could see it was impossible to dig the tractor out so he ran over to the P.U.D. guy and got there just as the driver of the big tractor was leaving (part of the miracle was that the driver had just plowed the road to the river). We have a gate on the river road that goes into the pasture where Glory was in the ice and if he had not plowed that section in the morning we would not have been able to get to her in time!

So, the P.U.D. fella drove the big tractor across the field, through the green patches and over some drifts to get to Glory. We had enough of the tow rope left to hook it to the scoop on the tractor.

Meanwhile, Glory was just sinking and she had totally stopped struggling and fighting. I was screaming at her at the top of my lungs and hitting her in the face. She would open those big, brown eyes and looked at us with great sadness. By now, he had the tow-rope hooked up to the tractor and began to lift Glory. She didn't even struggle. Then, he dragged her across the ice to where she could stand – and stand she did! She just stood right up, shook herself and that was it.

We walked her back to the barn and called the vet. After taking the wet blanket off her and putting a warm, dry blanket on her, I kept her moving in the round-pen. The very heavy winter blanket may have helped to save her life as well. Glory's whole body was one big frozen icicle, even under the blanket! The vet had brought a big, huge hair dryer and I brought my little hair dryer and towels and we rubbed and dried Glory as best we could. When she was pretty dry we put some big heavy winter blankets on her and got her moving and walking around, again. We were able to defrost everything on the horse but her tail. Would you believe it was one big, huge, long icicle? We had used the hair dryer on it and it was beginning to melt, but certainly was in no hurry. The vet looked at me and said "this is not going to thaw so do you have any scissors?" We cut the long hair off of Glory's tail just above her hocks. Glory came out of this whole bad experience with absolutely no problems except a very short, blunt, broom tail!

I look back and think "what if my daughter in law had not been there"? "What if we had not brought the yellow tow rope that my friend had in his car"? "What if the big tractor was not next door and what if they had not plowed the road earlier that day"? It could have been very bad for Glory, but I believe God put everything in place at the right time to help all of us.

And I have learned my lesson. When we have snow or snow drifts, the horses can stay in the dry runs. It's so much safer!

CHAPTER 19

"Star's Fight for Life"

Jeremiah 29:11 "For I know the thoughts that I have for you, says the Lord, thoughts of peace and not of evil to give you a future and a hope."

Now, back to my beautiful, bay Arab with the star on her forehead who had been through so much because of the lightning accident (with her horrible injury), she was stolen, had two difficult births and very serious physical complications.

You would think that would be enough for one horse and she would just live the rest of her life healthy and safe? On the other hand, you would think that would be enough fear, stress and trauma for one owner, but no, she continued to have more problems! As Forest Gump said, "Life is a box of chocolates and you never know what you're gonna get!" The good news is that God knows and He is always there, in the good times and bad. He makes everything beautiful IN HIS TIME. Not our time and sometimes not the way we want or prayed, but in the end it will always turn out for the best. *Ecclesiastes 3: 1-8 "To everything there is a season, a time for every purpose under heaven. A time to be born, and a time to die; a time to plant, and a time to pluck what is planted; a time to kill, and a time to heal; a time to break down, and a time to build up; a time to weep, and a time to laugh; a time to mourn, and a time to dance; a time to cast away stones, and a time to gather stones; a time to embrace, and a time to refrain from embracing; a time to gain, and a time to lose; a time to keep, and a time to throw away; a time to tear, and a time to sew; a time to keep silence, and a time to speak; a time to love, and a time to hate; a time of war, and a time of peace."*

I happened to notice Star when I looked out my window. She just did not look right because she was walking around circles. I went out to get a closer look and her body was all sweaty. That was enough for me and I immediately called my veterinarian!

Then I went to catch her so I could lead her and keep her moving. As I was waiting for the vet and walking Star, she kept trying to paw the ground which is a sign that she wants to lay down and roll. I could see in her eyes that she was in serious pain, but she was trying her hardest to obey me and follow.

Then it happened so quickly that I could not stop her! Star threw herself on the ground. She began thrashing around uncontrollably and banging her head on the ground. There was nothing I could do to stop her but pray that the vet would hurry and get here very soon. I have had horses colic before, but NEVER this violently.

Colic is not a disease in itself. It is a symptom that something inside of the horse is very wrong. Colic is a vitally important danger signal and can be mild or it can end in the death of the horse.

The vet finally arrived, and by now Star was up, but dripping wet with sweat. He began to examine her vitals and once again she violently threw herself on the ground and began rolling and thrashing about. He couldn't stop her from rolling until the pain subsided. Then he told me that it looked very serious, so he gave Star a big dose of sedative, injection for pain, then he put a rubber tube down her nose into her stomach (to run oil through her system so that anything blocking the intestinal tract could be loosened). She continued to be in distress and pain, so he had me bring her to the animal hospital. After I loaded her in the trailer, we went ahead and drove to the veterinary hospital. Meanwhile, I prayed that she wouldn't have another episode of severe pain in the trailer where she would fall down and get stuck or hurt. Thank God we made it the hospital with no problems!

We arrived at the hospital and I unloaded a very wet, sweaty horse, then I brought her into the examination room. They put her in a chute made of very sturdy round bars and secured her. Then several of the doctors that were there began to check her vitals, tap her under the belly and listen to see what they could hear inside of her. She was still doped-up from the earlier pain medicine that was given to her, but the fear and pain in her eyes was very obvious. The doctors did not look very hopeful.

Star's heart rate at that time, standing still, was 99 beats per minute. The normal heart rate of a horse just standing should be around 40 to 50 beats per minute. Sixty beats per minute is considered abnormal. A heart rate of over 80 beats is a very unfavorable sign. It often is seen during colics which can be fatal. It is a very serious condition. Heart rates over 200 beats per minutes have been recorded in race horses, but they recover and come down to under 70 beats per minute within 10 minutes. This is according to a book *"How to be your own Veterinarian"*. Star's heart rate was that high the whole time she was in the examining room, probably 20 minutes or more! After a long time, with different doctors examining Star, and nothing that seemed to change, I looked into Stars eyes and she was absolutely terrified. I know her and could read the fear in her, so, I asked the doctors if I could just take Star outside and walk her for a few minutes. They agreed that it would be okay, so, they freed her from the chute. I walked her outside and onto the grass. I just put my hand on her neck and began to pray for her that God would stop the pain and give Star peace so that she was not be so full of fear. I continued to pray and walk her around in the grass for about 15 minutes with no incident of her trying to throw herself to the ground. I brought her back and asked one of the veterinarians to come and check her out. He came and checked her pulse. It was down to 80 beats per minute. I walked her some more and continued to pray and then asked to have them check her again. This time her pulse was down to 60. Everyone was relieved but no one was more relieved than I! They listened to her belly and there were some gut sounds. That was a good sign because it meant that things inside of Star were beginning to work right again. Everyone was absolutely amazed because her symptoms were extremely serious and didn't look good at all. To have things turn around was indeed another miracle for Star! Her level of pain and high heart rate were signs of death, but once again, I believe God saved this beautiful bay mare with the star on her forehead. Some types of colic will plug the intestines and kill a horse. But, some colic can be operated on and that surgery will save the horse. To every horse owner "colic" is a deadly word and always scary. Later, I found a sack of old, rotten carrots in the barn that she must have eaten. Stress, food or any drastic change in the horse's life might cause colic.

I loaded Star into the trailer and took her home and she continues to live a normal horse's life. We have ridden her and enjoyed her. She is a wonderful horse!

CHAPTER 20

"Senior Star"

1 Peter 5:7"…cast all your care upon him for he cares for you."

The years have passed and Star is now a senor citizen - she is well over 30 years-old and that's old for a horse. Her eyes are still bright and beautiful, her coat is not quite as shiny and her withers stick up a little because her back is just slightly swayed. She is the boss with all the other horses and they respect her. She is the lead horse and they wait until she goes out in the pasture before they all go. If she pins her ears just slightly they back off quickly.

One morning not long ago I went down to feed the horses and since Star has a problem with founder (because of the retained afterbirth) I am careful of what she eats and always make sure that she doesn't get too much fresh, green grass. Someone suggested that I should only feed her pellets, which are made from orchard grass, because most other senior feeds are full of sugar and she can get fat. So I bought a bag of pellets which were made from orchard grass, like recommended. I noticed that the pellets were very big and hard, but they had been recommended by a very experienced horse person. So, I gave Star a small half of a scoop to begin with - probably only a half of a pound. I am always careful about changing feed, because horses can colic from changing their feed. I left Star and went on to feed the other horses and then clean the runs and the stalls. I had locked Star in the back stall so no one would bother her while she was eating. I went back to let her out when I saw this horrible look in her eyes and she was walking around and looking very nervous. I did not like what I saw because we have been there before and I did not want to go there again!

She began to paw the ground and I thought it looked like signs of colic and my heart just stopped! It had only been a half hour or less since I gave her the new pellets. I grabbed my cell phone and called my vet, Dr. Sauters, to see what he thought. Just as I was talking to him Star began to cough and green stuff began to come out of her nose and mouth. She coughed and coughed. I explained to the vet what she was doing and he said she had choked on the pellets and they were stuck in her throat. He said that it sounded like she was getting them out and clearing her throat because that green stuff coming out of her nose and mouth was a good sign. It looked scary to me!

I stayed with Star until she quit coughing and settled down a bit. Then I put her out in the moist grass to eat because of the dry feed that did not go down. I wanted all the moisture I could get to go down Star's throat. Thank

God this scary looking episode ended well and she was able to dislodge the pellets.

Once again, through the grace of God, Star won over a very difficult situation and I was, again, thanking God for saving my bay mare with the star on her forehead and her four white socks. What a life she has lived and what a drive to live she has! What a blessing to me she has been for all these years and what memories we have together. Our whole family considers Star a part of us and they all love her. She is a big part of our family. She represents the struggles of life and how much God cares and answers prayers for everyone. He loves ALL of His creation – even our beloved animals!

CHAPTER 21

"Fallen Tree"

Mark 4: 41 "…even the wind and the sea obey Him."

My husband, Ragnar, took me down to the lower barn by the hay field to show me a tree that was dead and leaning over the barn. He said he was going to have to use the tractor and tie a big rope to the tree to pull it back away from the barn before it fell across the barn and damaged the roof and stall under it. I am not sure how he was going to cut it down and make it fall backwards, but I figured he knows what he is doing. Then we both got busy and forgot about the dead, leaning tree!

Now it was the end of October and Ragnar was going north with some of his friends to have a time away in the wilderness of B.C. where they would minister to the natives in Bella Coola, leaving on a Friday. That night I had a party with the gals I ride with and we watched movies and had a great time.

On Monday the local news was predicting a bad storm coming with high winds. That evening as I was struggling against the wind while I was walking to the lower barn, the wind was howling against my face and pushing me backwards. I felt it was safer to keep the horses inside the barn. So, I put Star in her big 24'x24' stall in the back of the barn and then I remembered the leaning tree that Ragnar had spoken about! The wind was coming in mighty gusts right at the leaning tree pointing toward the barn *and* it was right over the stall where I had just put Star! There was no other stalls as big as that one for Star (she has difficulty getting up after laying down). So I just prayed out loud in the midst of the storm and asked Father God to please send His angels to hold up the tree so it would not fall on the barn and scare or injure Star. I also asked Him not to ruin the barn roof and stall. Star seemed to be okay. Emily was right there in the next stall and both horses seemed to be pretty quiet, even though the sounds the wind was making as branches crashed against the roof of the barn was awful. So, I turned the lights out and left the barn in the hands of God. He has stopped storms and walked on the water during storms. So what's a little wind storm of 60 or 70 miles an hour for God, Who created the wind? The Bible says that "nothing is impossible for God"!

That night as I watched the news they said we might be getting wind gusts of up to 60 miles and hour or more. Not good - as I sat there listening to the wind pounding our house when each huge wind gust would hit. I prayed again and asked God to intervene. I went to bed. What more could I do? Now it was in Gods hands.

The next morning when I went down to take care of Star, all was well! The leaning tree was still leaning. Now I began singing and rejoicing out loud in the barn, and the horses were wondering why I was so incredibly happy. I even put my arms around Star and gave her a big hug! I then scratched her really good and her lips wiggled with happiness.

The wind was still gusting and blowing. I went back to the house after feeding all the horses and sat down with a cup of coffee to hear the weather report. Once again they said we would have gusts and high winds all day. Late that afternoon when I struggled against the wind to walk to the lower barn, I could not believe what my eyes were seeing!

The leaning tree had fallen into many pieces to the west of the barn. It was leaning to the north and the wind was coming from the southwest. How did it fall away from the way it was leaning?

God is so good. Now I was really rejoicing because I didn't have to worry because of any windstorms. Boy, will Ragnar be happy. He just had to come home and pick up the pieces of a 'now broken tree' instead of cutting down a 'leaning tree over the barn'!

CHAPTER 22

"Relationship"

John 3:16 "For God so loved the world that He gave His only begotten Son, that whosoever believes in Him should not perish, but have everlasting life."

A friend of mine wanted her little 5 year-old daughter to ride Star and so she did. Star was so patient with her. They asked if they could have their daughter show her. I thought it was a great idea. So I thought I would show the little girl how to lead a horse with "showmanship". When I began to lead Star, her head was way up and she was dancing side ways which was not good. When I gave the lead rope to the 5 year-old, Stars head came down to the level of the little girl and she very gently walked as quiet as she could beside the little girl. What a horse! She knew this was a special, tiny person and she needed to be extra careful. They did show her and both did very well. I love her so much!

She will always be a part of our family. When my grandkids Jillian 8 and Kelson 5 come Star is always their first choice to ride. In fact, the people with the 5-year-old daughter wanted to buy Star, but our son Erik quickly said, "You cannot sell Star! She is family and will always be a part of our family." I knew that, but it was nice to hear it from one of our kids. Star is truly a miracle horse and reminds my family of the good times and the bad times we have all been through together. The hard times of losing everything and remembering back how God met our every need!

My prayer is that as you read this story it will give you hope that no matter what you face, the pain, the hurt, the rejection, the joy, or the laughter of life - that God is there and He does care! He cares about everything in your life, whether it is your finances, a job, loved ones, beloved animals or hobbies. He really wants to be a part of all our lives and enjoy life with us. If you like hiking in the mountains, thank Him for creating your eyes to the beauty as you hike. Perhaps you love motorcycles. Thank Him for the power of the motorcycle, the fun you have and the safety of His hands. If it's sports that you prefer, reading a good book, baking a cake or sewing a dress that you enjoy, thank Him for the time and the ability to do so.

Talk to God because He loves to hear your voice. In ***Psalm 139:4*** the Bible says ***"He knows all the words off your tongue before you even speak them."*** What's amazing is that He still loves us after hearing all of our foolish jabber!

When times are hard, as they are today, and uncertain just tell Him how you feel. Talk to God because He is there, waiting to listen. Pray and ask him for what you need. God always answers prayer, but it's always in His time and with His wisdom. His answer to our prayers may not always be how or when we want it, but He always knows best!

Romans 8:28 "For we know that all things work together for good, to those who love God and are called according to His purpose."

In that box of chocolates, life might be bitter and painful – it's not always sweet, but God's Word says in *Ecclesiastes 3:11 "He makes everything beautiful in its time"*.

Just living with this beautiful mare, Star, and watching her go through so many tragedies and be victorious over them all, is a blessing and encouragement. It's a blessing to me to know that God cares about my animals and has answered my prayers so many times. Sometimes, the answer was not what we wanted, like when we prayed that God would heal my beautiful mare, Mayim, who had broken her leg and was not healed. But, just a few years later, God brought me a miracle by replacing Mayim with Emily, who is her absolute mirror image!

And, who would've thought that an old mare like Nutmeg would like Mayim's two year-old son, Traveler! Never again did she even look at another stallion, but from then on, she only had eyes for Cisco. Again, that was God's timing and His plan.

There is one certainty in life and it is that someday, no matter what your age, you will die. There is no way to get around it! But we do have a choice about how we face death and what we think about it. Are you ready to choose Jesus? The joy of being a believer in Jesus Christ and making Him Lord of your life is that you have eternal life in Heaven forever and ever. In heaven there are no bad chocolates, no tears, sickness, disease, pain or fear. This earth is beautiful, but, it is nothing compared to heaven!

So, have you made Jesus Lord of your life and experienced His love for you? If you haven't received Him yet, talk to someone who knows Him. Get pointed in the direction of a relationship that will last forever and remember that the Bible (Basic Instructions Before Leaving Earth) is a roadmap for life's journey!

Let's close this book with a beautiful poem about God by

Beth Moore © (Reprinted and used by permission of Lifeway

Christian Resources).

He is Elohim creator, the omnipotent who rules,
He is the Sovereign King of Glory and earth is His footstool,
He is the Alpha and Omega, and the beginning and the End,
He sends forth lightning that later checks back in with Him!

He speaks worlds into existence and spins them out in space,

He gives orders to the morning and shows the dawn its place.

He prophecies the future then orders it fulfilled,

He bares fruit from a landscape that man has never tilled.

He feeds the beast of the field from the palm of His hand,

He watches while they bear their young and teaches them to stand.

He gives the seas their boundaries and hides its creatures deep,

He teaches eagles how to fly and nest upon the steep.

He makes the clouds His chariot and rides on wings of wind.

He champions the victim and brings proud men to end.

He is Emanuel God with us, come to earth through Christ,

He is the kinsman redeemer who paid the slave man's price.

He is the King of Kings; Lord of Lords and worthy is the Lamb,

He holds the keys to life eternal where the dead in Christ now stand.

He is enthroned between the cheribum and great is His reward,

The devil is His defeated foe, the weapon His swift sword.

The story has a moral so I'll hasten lest you tire,

Whoever you perceive He is,

You might aim a little higher!

By Beth Moore© (Reprinted and used by permission of Lifeway Christian Resources)

EPILOGUE

Last January during a very cold, snowy day my horses were coming into their stalls to be fed. It was then that I noticed that Ellie my big black and white mare (who is a half sister to Mayim and an aunt to Emily) was shaking all over. Ellie was big, fat and had a thick winter coat, so I knew that something was very wrong! I took her temperature and it was 104.5 degrees. That's high for a horse! I called Dr. Sauters and he came to my house immediately to examine the horse. He was also amazed at the high temperature. After a full examination he put Ellie on a strong shot of an antibiotics. I would have to give her two more shots in four days. We isolated her from the other horses and kept her in a box stall with the doors closed.

That same night my sweet Emily came in shaking and had a fever of 103.5 and so I called again and was able to run in and get her the shots. I gave them myself. The next day Spot, Emilie's half brother, came in shaking and had a fever and we began antibiotics with him and locked all three in separate stalls with the doors shut to the healthy horses. They remained isolated from all the other horses and in their stalls for 2 weeks. No other horses on the property came down with any symptoms. Even Star at 30 years old who was running with the three sick horses did not get sick. Thank God.

Several days later the wild mare Nutmeg came in but would not eat with the other horses. The next thing I knew she was kicking at her belly and rolling on the ground. She was collicking. I was helpless because I could not get near her. It would do no good to call a vet for her because no one could get close to her, even now, in this condition. The only thing to do was try and find someone from the Back County Horsemen with the experience of knowing how to shoot a horse. I was desperate and I could see she was in terrible pain. I felt helpless as the tears flowed down my face. I called the local chapter of BCH and they were so helpful. They gave me some numbers of people who they hoped could help. I tried calling and was having trouble getting anyone who was not at work or had other commitments. Now Nutmeg was on the ground struggling and in pain. I began to pray and call out desperately to God. I prayed for God to please not let her suffer any more; please, just end her pain and take her life. I watched hopelessly as she continued to struggle with the tears streaming down my face. I continued to pray and plead with God. Then Nutmeg took a big breath, blew it out and fell back flat on the ground and that was it. She stopped struggling. She was gone. I thanked God over and over for taking Nutmeg out of her pain. My husband Ragnar got the backhoe and buried her out in the woods in the back of the hay field where two baby horses are also buried. You would think that a horse who would never allow anyone to touch her or have any relationship with people would not be missed, but she still was my best brood mare, she did have her own personality and I really miss her!

I started this book over two years ago and had a really hard time finishing the book and getting it to the publisher. Spring finally came and summer tried to come, but in 2011 we really never had much of a summer. It seemed like things kept getting in the way of getting the book to the publisher. Finally, I decided that I would get up at 5:30 am. and get the whole book and pictures to Xulon Publishers. I was able to get it all in to them with the help of Janie McQueen, my editor, at about 6:00am. Wow! I had the greatest feeling of peace when it was finally all done. I mean real peace!

So, I went to feed the horses and get ready for my Monday prayer day. As I was getting ready for prayer the Lord prompted me to wear the necklace He gave me. You see, about 6 months ago a friend called and needed a ride to work. This friend loves Jesus with all her heart. She and her husband were on a mission trip to Peru several years ago and as she was walking along the street, the Lord spoke to her. He said to buy a necklace from a lady who was making them on the street. The lady was taking silver and beautiful jade stones and forming them into a gorgeous necklace. The Lord told my friend to buy that necklace and give it to the first person that tells her it is beautiful. So, I picked-up my friend and when we got to where she worked, she got out and turned to say thank you and my eye went to the necklace that she was wearing. I said to her that was the most beautiful necklace. She just stared at me and said nothing. Then she took the necklace off and handed it to me and shared the story that God told her to give it as a gift from Him. I just sat there as she left for work unable to move. I looked at the necklace in my hand and was completely overwhelmed. I am humbled at such love from a God who is so big and so Holy. He is the God that speaks and the stars are formed in the universe and yet He loves us humans in such a personal way! It's almost too much to understand but I believe it by faith. I finally got myself together and went to my prayer group. The gift was so personal that I just got by myself for a while and prayed, thanking God over and over for His love before I shared with the group of ladies that I pray with every Monday.

The reason I thought I was putting the necklace on that morning, after I got the book sent off, was for Israel and all that was going on in that country. I also wore my Star of David earrings that matched the necklace. We had a great prayer meeting and I came home to check on Star, as she has been fighting something (physically) for the last 2-3 months. Dr. Sharon Hoofnagle has been working with me and has been wonderful. She's been on the internet checking out what might work and calling other veterinarians for ideas to help Star get over the diarrhea that she has been fighting.

I found Star in the shadows of a tree in the hay field. I took her out into the sun for the warmth. She turned her backside to me. She has not done that for sometime now, and I scratched her backside. She turned and looked at me till she caught my eye and our eyes locked onto each others. She just stared at me and then I knew she was saying good-bye. Then, she walked back into the woods down the lane in the trees. I ran to call Dr. Hoofnagle. I ran back to her and Star was laying down. I got down in the dirt right next to her head, as I stroked her head and said good-bye, with tears freely flowing. I looked down and there was the necklace that the Lord gave me and I really melted then. I knew he prompted me to wear the necklace early that morning so that I would know He was with me in this very sad time. He knew Star was going home that day, and through the necklace, He reminded me of His love and care. God is so good. Star is now in Heaven in green pastures running freely with my horse Mayim and the old, wild mare, Nutmeg.

Once again, God is always with us in the good times and the bad times. He promised to never leave or forsake us. Do we have to do anything for that Love? No. God did it all by sending His only Son Jesus Christ to die on the cross and rise from the grave. He is alive and those who believe and have a relationship with Him, will be with Him forever and ever.

Biography

Rosemary Gustafson lives in Ferndale Washington with her husband Ragnar. They have 6 adult children (all married) from a "blended" family and 8 grandchildren. Rosemary is a graduate of Whitworth College in Spokane, Washington and taught school for several years. The last 30 or more she has been raising horses and now they own a horse boarding stable called Son Shine Ranch where she and her husband work. To reach Rosemary for speaking or book signing please contact Rosemary at sonshinelighthouse@msn.com

Books can be ordered through Xulon Press:
1-866-909-2665

And the website: www.xulonpress.com